Praise for

BEYOND BUSYNESS

"Too many people have fallen into the busy cycle that Peggy so accurately and honestly portrays. This book is the wakeup call you need to get back to living."

—**Seth Godin,** author of *The Song of Significance*

"As a certifiable 'Busyness addict,' I totally relate to Peggy Sullivan's story. I only wish I'd had her research sooner. *Beyond Busyness* is the framework you need to help you balance being productive with what matters most to you."

—**Mel Robbins,** *New York Times* bestselling author and host of *The Mel Robbins Podcast*

"When did 'Busy' become an answer to 'How are you?'? Good question! And Peggy Sullivan has answers, born of her own journey, that drive home the terrible costs of Busyness. Armed with data, Sullivan shows that addiction to Busyness is a pathology eating away the happiness and health of far too many of us nowadays and provides actionable steps for overcoming it. Honest and practical, *Beyond Busyness* is for anyone longing for more clarity, focus, and meaning in their lives."

—**Amy C. Edmondson,** Novartis Professor of Leadership, Harvard Business School, and author of *Right Kind of Wrong*

"Being busy and 'getting things done' feels great. But as Peggy Sullivan says in this urgent and necessary book, Busyness is not the secret to success. We're all searching for the holy grail of balancing productivity with happiness. *Beyond Busyness* might just be it."

—**Eric Schurenberg,** former CEO, *Inc.* and *Fast Company*

"In this important book, Peggy Sullivan reveals the many hidden dangers of Busyness and how to combat them to live a better life."

—**David Meerman Scott,** marketing strategist and author of thirteen books, including *The New Rules of Marketing and PR*

"Busyness is not a badge of honor—it keeps us from becoming who we were made to be and achieving our highest potential. *Beyond Busyness* provides actionable solutions to the world's epidemic of time poverty. It's a fun read that helps eliminate the distracting noise around us so we can step into our power."

—**David Nurse,** NBA development coach, *Wall Street Journal* bestselling author, and worldwide keynote speaker

"Time is too precious to waste it being busy! In this engaging book, Peggy Sullivan shows how to move beyond the Busyness, reclaim your life, and make time for what really matters."

—**Laura Vanderkam,** author of *Tranquility by Tuesday*

"*Beyond Busyness* emphasizes the importance of values—and specifically connection—as the secret sauce that enables a bond, a relationship, and trust like no other. Connectors are the ones I want in my foxhole when the going gets tough. Values management is yesterday's time management. Today, it's about focusing on what is important."

—**Erik Qualman,** bestselling author of *Digital Leader* and *Socialnomics*

"In *Beyond Busyness*, Peggy Sullivan passionately emphasizes the paramount importance of intentionally prioritizing and wholeheartedly focusing on what truly matters. Don't be too busy to read it—you need it!"

—**Didi Wong,** serial entrepreneur and angel investor, producer, mentor, and philanthropist

"Through her innovative three-step Busy-Busting Process, Peggy Sullivan provides practical, actionable solutions that encourage us to rethink our approach to work and life. Her strategies are designed not only to enhance productivity but also to foster happiness and well-being. Since reading her book, I've shifted my way of being and realigned how I feel and show up. It's all about taking microsteps and changing our own operating systems. Her book is the best Busyness addiction recovery program."

—**Saleema Vellani,** keynote speaker, award-winning author, and founder and CEO of Ripple Impact

"Just when the pandemic made us realize how overworked we have become, making us want to shout the quiet-quitting motto, 'Stop the world, I want to get off,' Peggy Sullivan rescues us from our self-made work-prisons with *Beyond Busyness*. Her message, that work and life can be more enjoyable when we do less, will undoubtedly bring more fulfillment to those stuck in live-to-work quagmires."

—**Dr. Irwin Gellman,** director of research, Roswell Park Cancer Institute

"When I work with someone who is always dealing with emergencies in a business context, my first impression is that they are not the best planners. It's then when I am very tempted to share Peggy's Busy-Busting Process— Subtraction: Eliminate low-value things that you can easily delegate. Your time is a lot more valuable when you do things that matter. Mojo Making: Now that time is on your side, you will work on things that have better and higher returns, which is very rewarding and creates an influx of endorphins translating to happiness. The happier you are with what you do, the more value you will add. Values Vibing: Once you have the gift of more time and happiness, you'll find that time is a canvas that you paint with your values."

—**German Santana,** digital marketing executive, Google

BEYOND BUSYNESS

www.amplifypublishinggroup.com

Beyond Busyness: How to Achieve More by Doing Less

For more information, please contact:
Amplify Publishing, an imprint of Amplify Publishing Group
620 Herndon Parkway, Suite 220
Herndon, VA 20170
info@amplifypublishing.com

Library of Congress Control Number: 2024909666

CPSIA Code: PRV0624A

ISBN-13: 979-8-89138-265-7

Printed in the United States

To anyone who is stuck

on the hamster wheel of Busyness

and wants more out of life.

PEGGY SULLIVAN

Beyond Busyness

How to Achieve MORE by Doing LESS

amplify
an imprint of Amplify Publishing Group

CONTENTS

INTRODUCTION

Hi. My name is Peggy, and I'm a recovering Busyness addict. Yes, that's right. I am addicted to *being busy*. And although I have now overcome it, most of the time, it has been a long and difficult journey to recovery.

Like many addicts, it took me years to even realize I had a problem. I used to wear my packed schedule like a badge of honor. I loved telling people how busy I was. I had lots of wake-up calls, but none of them woke me up. Here are a few of the more exciting ones:

- Destroyed my marriage
- Totaled my car
- Superglued my hands together
- Nearly died from a heart attack
- Accidentally ate cat food, mistaking it for pistachios

- Missed the grand opening event for my nonprofit organization
- Tipped a waiter $300,000 instead of $30
- Went to a big speaking event wearing two different shoes (thankfully, just one on each foot)

And this is just the most dramatic stuff. I was a highflier, a massive achiever, and yet I had no life. I wandered around in a burned-out haze. I wasn't healthy, happy, or focused on what's important.

My always-on lifestyle led me in every direction *but the one I truly wanted to follow.*

Busyness controlled me!

But then I finally learned how to control it.

After spending decades drowning in Busyness myself, and years more researching it in the people around me, I discovered a simple yet powerful truth:

When we do less, we become more.

I have also learned that most struggle to experience this truth. In fact, more than three out of four people I have surveyed in my annual study on this topic feel overwhelmed by Busyness and have no clear idea how to escape the cycle.

Thankfully, I have also discovered something else: a methodology to help people like you overcome Busyness and *actually live a happy and satisfying life while getting stuff done.*

Today, I'm a keynote speaker, trainer, and thought leader with the mission of sharing this methodology to help move the world past the damaging false belief that busy is the secret to success.

Let me be clear: Busy is *not* that secret. It is, in fact, absolutely the opposite.

If you're realizing that endless hustle isn't the road to fulfillment and being busy all the time *limits* what you're achieving far more than it contributes but you can't seem to figure out what to do about it—then this book is for you.

This book will help you turn your *hustle culture* into *productive and happy culture.*

It will help you *choose meaning over mayhem* in both your career and private life.

And I promise you, I am the perfect companion for this voyage because *I will not stop* until this culture shift and this choice are available to all of us.

My research-backed strategies have helped Fortune 500 companies such as Google, Bank of America, and Blue Cross Blue Shield get their people off the busy treadmill and change the way they align their time with their values.

They have also helped many small companies and individuals. I have seen the radical transformation that members of my nonprofit, SheCAN!, have experienced over time while consistently using these techniques.

And now I am sharing my methodology in this book so I can help you and people like you overcome the world's culture of Busyness and find something much better.

My research has been both qualitative and quantitative. I have conducted surveys via my organization SheCAN! I have also had in-depth conversations with colleagues and acquaintances. Many of the stories I highlight throughout this book come from casual conversations with people whom I would even call friends. All the stories are real and true.

Finding such stories is not difficult. Almost everyone I meet is fighting to get to the other side of Busyness.

Going Beyond Busyness takes vision and endurance. Like any journey it demands you set out in the right direction and be committed to get to the end of it.

I have taken that journey, and not just once. Today, I keep taking that journey, guiding people like yourself across those wide waters, and lending a life preserver, a long stick, or my hand if necessary to keep you from drowning. I'm not special or better. I've just been across these waves before.

You, too, may have tried this journey before—going from busy as your life purpose to busy as a memory. If you didn't make it across, or fell backward, take heart—we can do this together.

If you haven't yet figured out that your Busyness is a crippling addiction, keep reading.

I am looking forward to hearing about your journey. Your life will never be the same when you make it to the other shore: Beyond Busyness.

CHAPTER 1

BUSY IS A FOUR-LETTER WORD

"Cardiac arrest!"

As the ambulance rushed me to the hospital, the paramedic's voice on the radio swirled above me in circles. I heard these two words again and again like it was a mantra I was practicing to keep myself breathing.

How could this be happening to me? I am healthy. I eat well. I exercise. I work on things that make the world work better. I get tons done. I am a very *busy* person.

Only an hour earlier, I had been attending a typical big work meeting for my job as marketing director at Blue Cross Blue Shield. We had meetings like this all the time, and I participated with energy and enthusiasm, like a powerful leader should.

Ironically, since it is a health-care company, there were plenty of doctors and nurses in the room. And just a few minutes into the meeting, I noticed everyone was staring at me. Was the button on my blouse undone? Did I have coffee stains on my blazer or something?

No, apparently, I was turning blue. Dr. Lee, who was sitting next to me, leaned over and asked me, "Are you OK? Your pupils are dilated."

As I started to answer, I felt a stabbing pain in my chest and could not complete my breath to speak. Then I collapsed. And the next thing I knew, I was having what felt like a heart attack.

In the hospital, I could barely sleep. I kept thinking, "A heart attack at the age of forty? How is this possible?" It turned out it was a minor stress-related heart attack. After three days, they discharged me. I was so glad to be released, not only because it meant I was OK but also because I could get back to my life. I had way too much going on to spend time in a hospital bed.

Indeed, as soon as I got home, I went right back to my basic cycle—*eat, work, sleep, repeat*. With a whole bunch of being a single mother thrown in as well.

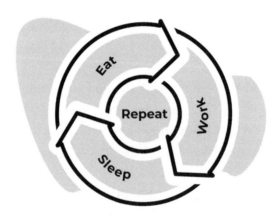

I didn't yet realize that Busyness was not the solution to having too much to do. Busyness was actually the central problem, the key cause of all this mess.

Therefore, the solution was simple—*stop being busy.*

Easier said than done, of course. In today's world, who can stop being busy even for fifteen minutes?

My heart attack happened twenty years ago. I saw the truth then and many times since. Now I've written a whole book, which you have started reading, about how low-value and unintentional Busyness is bad and how we need to focus on what is important. But I still struggle to slow down and focus on what matters.

I have lived most of my life in an endless cycle of eat, work, sleep, repeat.

Well, in my case it has usually been more like *mother, eat, mother, work, mother, sleep, mother. Repeat.*

Because working mothers are the busiest people on the planet.

And here's the strange thing: I loved, and love, eating, sleeping, working, and mothering. I absolutely love them to bits. And yet the combination of one after another, without a break, was literally killing me.

You would think a heart attack would have delivered the message once and for all. But as you'll soon see, it didn't. In today's world, "busy" is the only four-letter word that we think means the opposite. It's the only curse word we actually think describes something desirable.

We think being busy is a great thing, so it's often the last place we look when trying to solve our life challenges. The rest of this chapter will show you that it's the first place we should be looking.

BUSY ALMOST KILLED ME (MORE THAN ONCE)

Just a few months before my heart attack, I already thought my life couldn't get worse. My best friend, Ray, my husband of twenty-two

years, father to our twelve-year-old son, Brandon, decided to celebrate Christmas Eve by telling me he needed a time-out from our
marriage. It wasn't working for him anymore.

In fact, as far as he was concerned, there wasn't much of a marriage left. I was absent too much, even when I was around. I was
way too busy for his liking. I was disconnected from him and what
was important to our marriage. And I had been for a long time.

Eat, work, sleep, repeat.

It may seem absurd to say that his timing was terrible. What
divorce is timed well? But it could not have been timed worse. Brandon was going to have his bar mitzvah in a few short months. We
had planned the celebration for over a year.

Hundreds of friends and family were coming. Everyone had
bought their flight tickets. We had paid for the party, the musicians,
the photographers, and Brandon's first grown-up suit. Now the event
would be more like the coming-out party for my failed marriage.

My friends couldn't believe it either. Ray was Prince Charming
as a lover, generous as a partner, a remarkable father. What the
heck was wrong with me? His Aunt Betty used these words exactly:
"What did you do to destroy your perfect storybook life?"

Looking back, it seems I should have gotten the point right
then. But somehow I still blamed it all on him. Betty's question
about my responsibility in this offended me. I was a hardworking
and extremely loving woman. He left me anyway. It couldn't be *me*.
Prince Charming just became a frog all of a sudden.

Soon, he moved out, to go hang out with the other frogs in
some other pond, I guess. His time-out became permanent, and he
never came back.

It took a heart attack for me to start seeing the reality I had
already sensed for decades: Busy is not about having a lot to do. Busy

is not actually about doing at all. It is a way of being. It is an adjective that describes identity, not actions.

Busyness was not about me living my life in a full, rich way. Busyness was keeping me from living my best life. Busy kept me distracted and blinded, so I couldn't see that my life was disintegrating in front of my eyes.

The collapse of my marriage and my heart attack were just two crises. There were so many more. All of it stemmed from a series of actions that, alone, were wonderful and fulfilling but resulted in a recurring mantra:

Eat, work, sleep, mother, repeat.

I was chasing shiny candy like a kid on Halloween. My life had become a series of meetings, emails, and work events that pretended to be social but weren't. Most of the meetings were pointless, but I was sure I had to be there, and so were my employers. These often meaningless transactions left me no time to think, be creative, or plan for the big picture.

Ray leaving me didn't slow me down. My heart attack didn't slow me down. In fact, they both sped me up. When I got tired of the endless whirlwind, I just kept on whirling. Because that's what today's woman should do.

Sleep? Not important. Exercise? When I could fit it in.

Meals? An exercise in multitasking, scoring my speed of shoving food between my lips against the measure of how many emails I could reply to.

Every minute of my life was scheduled. But I couldn't be bothered to schedule fifteen inviolable minutes for my family or myself.

I couldn't keep living like this.

Friends and colleagues said, "You need to find some work-life balance, Peggy!" And I tried, but it never worked.

Later, I learned the reason it never worked is that work-life balance is an absurd idea. First, work isn't the opposite of life; it's part of it. Second, I've never met anyone who honestly believes that this "balance" is remotely possible.

When opportunity knocks professionally, it's important to lean in before that door closes. When you have a sick child, you need to be there regardless of what you had planned. We don't balance work and not work. We have to sacrifice one for the other. We need to make hard choices sometimes. We need to say, "Hey, I worked seven evenings in a row. Let me be home for the eighth, no matter what my boss thinks."

We're all distracted by candy. But as a mother I know the dangers of strangers offering candy. Just because everyone is doing something doesn't mean it's good.

WE HAVE ALL COME UNDONE

Los Angeles has twenty streets longer than fourteen miles. The infamous Sunset Boulevard is more than twenty miles long. Sepulveda, Mulholland, and Figueroa are all even longer. I know this because my friend Lisa walked up and down these streets for hours, looking for her car. Well, not even her car. Losing her own car would be bad enough, but this was her company's car, with weeks of work sitting in stacks on the back seat.

I would say she should have seen it coming. She did. In our weekly conversations, she told me again and again, "Life is hectic, but I'm managing, and it will get better soon."

But instead, what happened soon was that her mother became very sick and required a triple bypass. Lisa made sure she was there for her mother. Taking half a day off work to be there for the operation wasn't easy, but she managed. And the next day she was even able to make her work appointments, which were mostly near the hospital, so she could visit her mother. It all seemed to be working somehow. Until she went outside and couldn't find the car.

Months of nonstop activity had set her up to become a mindless zombie. Her mother's crisis snapped her across the edge. She had already spent hours searching for her car when she called me for advice, even though I was across the country in Buffalo. I wasn't the first person she called and probably not the last. But who could possibly help?

She finally found the car the next day, but the damage was done. Her boss was furious she had missed so many meetings and demanded she make up for it. And soon, it was Lisa who became sick. All the stress developed into a blistery rash that took months to get rid of.

What's the point of this story? Lisa thought she could manage living her life on the knife's edge, until her mother's situation threw her just a little off-balance.

Stop Focusing on the Unimportant—Spend Your Time on What Matters.

Because it isn't just Lisa. Not by a long shot. I have noticed more and more over the past few years how often friends and colleagues answer my question, "How are you doing?" with the absurd response, "I'm so busy!"

Have you noticed this when you ask the same question to the people in your life? When did "busy" become an answer to "How are you?"?

When we ask "How are you?" an automatic response such as "Fine" doesn't really answer the question with any depth. "Busy!" is far worse. It doesn't describe a "how" at all. It doesn't provide any information about well-being or state of mind. It just means you are doing a lot.

When I realized how many of my friends and colleagues were answering "busy" to the simple question of how they are, I decided to start counting the number of people who were saying this. I'm a data-driven person who feels strongly that to understand something, you first have to measure it. And I discovered that fully 94 percent of people answered "busy" when I asked them how they were doing.

This made me so concerned that I decided to run a more formal survey. I even hired a research firm to help. The surveyed people ranged across all types: young and old, single and married, male and female, working and unemployed.

In this more formal environment, people may have been a bit less frank. Still, fully 76 percent of the respondents indicated that they were "busy" or "very busy"—and that they really would like to be less busy than they were. Men and women were pretty much equal in this, with a difference of only 1 percent. Two-thirds of the respondents said they were "surviving, not thriving."

What this survey revealed, quite strongly, is a simple truth. As much as we all love *saying* we are busy, we don't like *feeling* busy or *behaving* busy.

A total of 74 percent in the survey said they were experiencing feelings of burnout, while 64 percent found self-care to be a challenge. More than half said they found it difficult to get even one good night's sleep because of their Busyness. Additionally, 43 percent of people said they found it difficult to focus, 60 percent said they were at least partly unhappy, and nearly 70 percent said they needed to improve their level of happiness. And yet 86 percent—a vast majority—said they believed happiness brings important benefits.

The charts that follow are a more comprehensive look at the results.

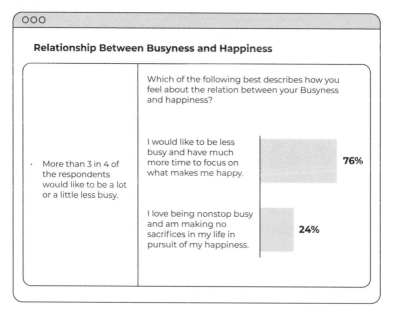

Relationship Between Busyness and Happiness

Which of the following best describes how you feel about the relation between your Busyness and happiness?

- More than 3 in 4 of the respondents would like to be a lot or a little less busy.

I would like to be less busy and have much more time to focus on what makes me happy.   **76%**

I love being nonstop busy and am making no sacrifices in my life in pursuit of my happiness.   **24%**

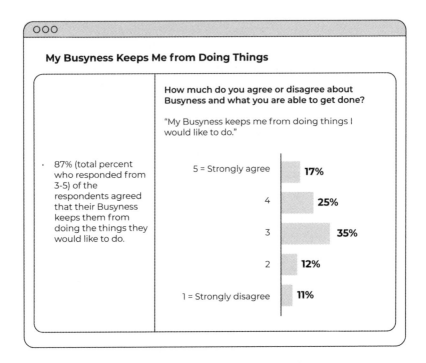

I have repeated this survey now four years in a row and made it more comprehensive each time. The results are always similar.

As a successful woman with a long corporate background, I've noticed that the number one challenge women indicate in this survey is not having time for what's important. They feel time poor. A total of 87 percent in the survey said they do not have time for what's important. Time poverty is a real thing, even though, of course, we all have the same amount of time available to us.

My friend Carolyn Gitlin agrees. As the chair of National Women's Philanthropy for the Jewish Federations of North America, she interacts with a lot of women and sees how so many are stuck in a cycle of Busyness.

She told me, "Our society glamorizes Busyness. People have this desire to consistently develop and grow, and a lot of people are competitive. So they strive and drive and turn it out and constantly keep climbing. People don't know how to turn it off. Busy is bad. It's a four-letter word. *Ughh.*"

BUSY IS BAD ON SO MANY LEVELS

I couldn't see anything as my car flipped. I could only feel myself skidding upside down and hear the sound of glass smashing.

When I woke up, there were firemen trying to get me out of the car using the jaws of life. My first thought wasn't about my health. My first thought was "I don't have time for this."

That's how busy I was.

I had been on my way to the first major event for my nonprofit, SheCAN!, which I will tell you about later in this book. This was an event I had planned for nine months, sweated over, and spent a whole lot of money on.

I looked at my watch. Seriously, I did not have time for this accident. But there I was, trapped inside bent metal. There could be no metaphor that more aptly described the Busyness trap in which I found myself.

Glancing at my watch, I realized the event was starting in fifteen minutes. I couldn't stomach not being there. I had spent the entire morning practicing my speech, and I had sorted out every tiny detail, including those I should have delegated, such as printing the name tags.

I had gotten my hair and makeup done. Now I was covered in blood, and when I tried to shout at the firemen to hurry up, noise barely came out. It was my hair's fault. My makeup's fault. They caused me to run late. It had nothing to do with *me*.

I really did blame my hair. I hadn't had a proper styling in months, so I thought it was fair to treat myself. But of course, I could only find time at the last minute. The salon ran an hour behind, and I had to rush home to dress. My brand-new dress sandals that I didn't have time to try on in the shop had a wonky backstrap that got stuck on the gas pedal. There was no time to stop the car to fix it. Besides, I could do it while driving. Why not?

Now I know why not. I was imprisoned in the bent metal for quite some time, enough to also blame my dress and my shoes. While the firemen were trying to pry me out, I was still probing with bloodstained fingers to call Mary Anne, the vice president of SheCAN!, to tell her I was on my way and not to start without me.

But they did start without me—in fact, I missed the entire event. It took them over an hour to get me out of the car, and then I discovered I was covered in blood.

HOCUS-POCUS THERE'S NO FOCUS!

Later, in my hospital bed, I realized it was Busyness, not my hair or my dress or my shoe, that caused this very costly accident. Forget about my bruises, my clothes, or my totaled car. I missed the launch of my own organization that I had dedicated months to setting up. And I missed it because of my Busyness in trying to execute it.

This all happened several years after my heart attack. I had learned nothing. Like a recalcitrant toddler who goes back to climb a high shelf she was warned away from, I couldn't let go of Busyness. When we are busy trying to catch up with our future, we miss out on the present.

There are so many bad impacts of Busyness.

- **BUSYNESS DESTROYS QUALITY THINKING**
Over 90 percent of people in the survey said that being busy affected their ability to think clearly at work, their ability to prioritize, the quality of their work, and also how innovative or creative they are. A total of 50 percent of people said that it "often" affected their time for important, long-term projects, while 49 percent indicated that it often affected their time for quality thinking at work.

- **BUSYNESS ENCOURAGES SMALL-PICTURE REASONING**
A total of 44 percent reported that Busyness often impairs their ability to see the bigger picture or think strategically, and 46 percent said that it often robs them of time needed to develop their team. One of the problems with being a high-achiever is that the minute we achieve something, we feel the need to justify the achievement by delivering results.

  I get a promotion, and I don't take the time to celebrate it—I realize that my boss wants me to show him that he made the right call in promoting me. So we are constantly focusing on the next step instead of the big vision.

- **BUSYNESS ADDS TO STRESS**
A total of 49 percent of people said that being busy "often" impacts their ability to switch off, 47 percent reported that it often elevates their stress levels, and 42 percent mentioned that it often has a harmful effect on their sleep.

In one of my first jobs, I knew a type A personality who loved to say "There's time for sleep when I'm dead." At the time I liked that phrase a lot. I knew what he meant: Sleep is for the weak. Efficiency is important above all else.

We strive to be as efficient as possible, even in our exercise. Our goal is to get in and out of the gym as quickly as we can, doing a routine that gives us the fastest results with the least effort. Exercise is something we check off the list. We make sure it happens. Same with decent rest. This is stressful.

- **BUSYNESS ELICITS EMOTIONAL DISTRESS**
  Emotional distress due to Busyness manifests as difficulty focusing and concentrating, impatience and irritability, trouble getting adequate sleep, and mental and physical fatigue. This is a vicious cycle, of course. Emotional distress leads to trouble with sleep and fatigue, which leads to more distress.

- **BUSYNESS HURTS FRIEND AND FAMILY DYNAMICS**
  Statistics indicate that 75 percent of parents are too busy to read to their children at night. Busyness affects romance and causes divorce. It results in less time for a partner and less time for self—which causes stress and burnout.

Being busy destroys our physical and mental health, alienates us from our relationships, and damages the quality of our work. We make bad decisions. We experience burnout. We forget how to focus.

A recent study by Microsoft shows that the attention span of the human race has dropped by one-fourth in the last few years. We can now only focus on average for eight and a half seconds, representing a 50 percent decrease compared with twenty years ago.*

Our memories are still slightly better than a goldfish, but our attention span is now shorter. That's not a joke. That's a fact.

Dr. Miriam Zylber, a mental health physician at a leading Miami hospital, says it succinctly: "We suffer from being busy, but we don't understand the price we pay."

BUSY DOESN'T EVEN WORK —IT'S THE ENEMY OF ACCOMPLISHMENT

My friend Jane considered herself a master of time management. She could multitask with the best of them and get it all done. Yet she arrived very late for one of the most important appointments of her life. She really thought she would make it on time. Even if she was a few minutes late, so what? Being late caused her to miss a very important moment in her son's life.

He ran sixty-three yards on one of the first plays of his first football game and scored his first touchdown. When he was celebrating in the end zone, looking around, she wasn't there. "Hey, no problem," he told her. But he was just being a typical teenager. Of course, it was a problem.

Jane felt terrible. But there was no way she could ever make up for it. She watched it again and again on the video replay. But that

---

* "How Long Can the Brain Focus? The Science of Focus," Brainelevate, last updated October 4, 2022, https://brainelevate.com/how-long-can-the-brain-focus/.

didn't help. She could feel better all she wanted. But it was her son who was hurt.

Being busy doesn't just damage ourselves. It also creates stress for everyone around us, both at work and in our personal lives. We leave people we care about feeling ignored or neglected. We grow distant without even noticing it.

In our survey, nearly eight of ten women said that "family" is the source of their happiness. And yet they have almost no time available for family—roughly the same number of respondents said that family commitments are part of what makes them too busy. Checking boxes does not mean we're happy. Filled in is not fulfilled.

The typical response to having a lot to do is to use time management techniques: calendar reminders, notifications, time blocking. The problem is, managing time doesn't make more of it. Every time we cross something off that to-do list (*Kaching!*), we add three more. Often, crossing a task off *requires* adding further tasks first.

Perhaps the most common technique of time management is multitasking. A total of 62 percent in our survey said multitasking was their key strategy to overcome their Busyness. It was by far the most popular answer.

Yet study after study shows that multitasking doesn't work. In fact, it radically undermines our efficiency. Multitasking literally splits the brain in two, forcing the left and right hemispheres to work independently, reducing productivity by as much as 40 percent. A study from Watson and Strayer[*] shows that only 2.5 percent

---

[*] Jason M. Watson and David L. Strayer, "Supertaskers: Profiles in Extraordinary Multitasking Ability," *Psychonomic Bulletin & Review* 17, no. 4 (2010): 479–85, https://doi.org/10.3758/PBR.17.4.479.

of people—one out of forty of us—are able to multitask effectively. For the rest of us, multitasking makes us take almost three times as long to get the job done, with three times as many errors.[*]

Multitasking leads to lower GPAs for college students[†] and IQ score declines of up to 15 points, lowering an adult's intelligence to the level of an eight-year-old.[‡]

Even in the rare moments that multitasking does work, the stretch it takes to get there leaves you *feeling* as though you weren't productive, which takes a toll on your mental health. The more often people in one study were interrupted by emails and task switching, the more likely they were to say they didn't feel productive, no matter what the results were.[§]

Just having access to our emails increases our stress levels noticeably even if we don't check them.[¶] In other words, knowing

---

[*] Sylvain Charron and Etienne Koechlin, "Divided Representation of Concurrent Goals in the Human Frontal Lobes," *Science* 328, no. 5976 (2010): 360–3, https://doi.org/10.1126/science.1183614.

[†] Saraswathi Bellur, Kristine L. Nowak, and Kyle S. Hull, "Make It Our Time: In Class Multitaskers Have Lower Academic Performance," *Computers in Human Behavior* 53 (2015): 63–70, https://doi.org/10.1016/j.chb.2015.06.027.

[‡] Christian P. Janssen, Sandy J.J. Gould, Simon Y.W. Li, Duncan P. Brumby, and Anna L. Cox, "Integrating Knowledge of Multitasking and Interruptions across Different Perspectives and Research Methods," *International Journal of Human-Computer Studies* 79 (2015), https://doi.org/10.1016/j.ijhcs.2015.03.002.

[§] Gloria Mark, Shamsi Iqbal, Mary Czerwinski, and Paul Johns, "Focused, Aroused, but so Distractible: A Temporal Perspective on Multitasking and Communications (2015), https://www.microsoft.com/en-us/research/wp-content/uploads/2016/10/p903-mark.pdf?utm_source=zapier.com&utm_medium=referral&utm_campaign=zapier.

[¶] Kostadin Kushlev and Elizabeth W. Dunn, "Checking Email Less Frequently Reduces Stress," *Computers in Human Behavior* 43 (2015): 220–28, https://doi.org/10.1016/j.chb.2014.11.005.

there is more to do that is not related to what you are currently doing is very distracting for humans.

So why is time management still so popular? Well, it's a multibillion-dollar industry, for one thing. And I guess it works for a few people. But it doesn't work for the people in our survey. Time management does not leave time for self-care, family, friends—the things that really matter. Being busy might mean doing more, but it doesn't mean getting more done.

"BUSY" IS A FOUR-LETTER WORD—FOR REAL

When I was a little girl, words like f*** and s*** were not allowed in our house. If we said them, our dad would literally wash out our mouth with soap. Then he would give us a big glass of water so we could blow bubbles to make it seem a bit more fun and less drastic.

This might seem like child abuse in today's context. And some may argue that punishment is not the best way to teach positive values. But the lesson I am pointing at here is that the words we use matter. And whatever method we use to do it, the same way we want to teach our children not to utter all the other curse words, we need to teach them, and ourselves, to banish "Busy" from our vocabulary.

We use "Busy" to make ourselves feel better because somehow, we've all come to hear this word as a badge of honor, a status symbol.

- *Oh, you're busy? You must be successful and important.*

- *If a doctor has a six-month waiting list, they must be worth waiting for.*
- *If an employee works overtime and all weekend, they must be a rock star.*

"How are you?"

"Busy!"

Wash Your Mouth Out!

"Busy" is a metaphor for achievement tinged by a curse. Unlike "Fine," it actually means something. But not something good. It suggests self-satisfaction from drowning in overwhelm. Elation from being flooded in misery. Pride shown off by apology. It's a humble-brag, show-off, and plea for help all rolled into one. We're on the edge of burnout, but don't worry, we'll never collapse. We're in action, we're dealing with it, and soon, very soon, it will all calm down.

"I'm doing great. And terrible. I have no time."

Describing your panic as "busy" doesn't make it better. In fact, the closest accurate meaning for "busy" is another four-letter word: "Help!"

We need to start hearing the word "busy" for what it actually is: a swear word. A profanity. Every time we catch ourselves saying the word "busy," we need to wash our mouth out with metaphorical soap.

Next time someone asks how you are, find a different way to describe yourself. You may struggle to find good words to replace "busy." That's all right. It's easier said than done. For me, it soon became clear that Busyness was more than a bad habit. It was an addiction.

BUSY-BUSTING TOOL #1

Wash Your Mouth Out

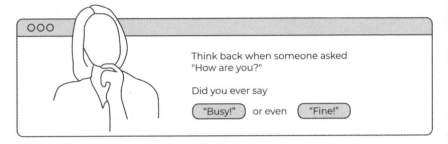

Think back when someone asked "How are you?"

Did you ever say

"Busy!" or even "Fine!"

Take a few minutes to make a list of other more genuine and generous responses you could have given.

In the next few days, use these or similar ways of answering the "How are you?" question. Actually, stop for a moment, connect with the person, and say something meaningful.

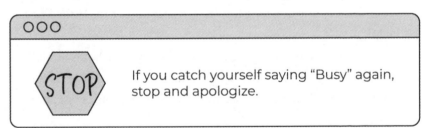

STOP

If you catch yourself saying "Busy" again, stop and apologize.

Begin to train yourself to manage this conversation differently.

Whenever you even think of the word "Busy," start to taste the remnants of Ivory soap in your mouth and say something else. Anything else!

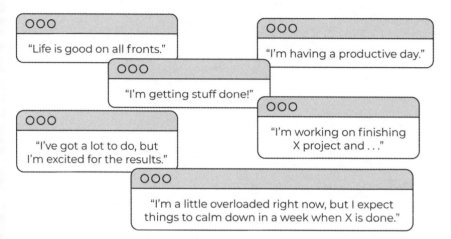

It's hard to find a professional who doesn't feel stressed, busy, tired, or overworked. Dropping these responses from your vocabulary, except when they're truly needed, will make you feel calmer and appear more capable to others and to yourself.

So let's practice:

How are you? Fill in the blank!

CHAPTER 2

BUSYNESS IS AN ADDICTION

I remembered that my life was too busy yet again when I woke up sprawled ass up on my couch with my cat, Dazzle, gagging inches from my face, spasming in slow motion.

Moments later, he vomited right next to my face. He threw up a pile of pistachio nuts. Then, disturbed by a stray thought, I looked down to my fist and opened it. Sure enough, cat kibbles. I was so exhausted I fed Dazzle my salty nuts and ate his dry food instead.

I wished I could also vomit, not because I had eaten cat food but because deep in the pit of my stomach, I realized how insane and unmanageable my life had gotten—again.

This was *five* years after my husband left me, and after my heart attack. *Five years* more had gone by, and here I was all over again, letting my busy schedule destroy me and even my cat. Never mind what this must have been doing to my son, who was eighteen years old now. What was I teaching him?

I had taken that job at Blue Cross, and a couple of months earlier, the government issued a rule book changing the landscape for health-care companies, including what we could and couldn't do in marketing. And since I was responsible for all the marketing materials, I had to do everything again and again.

I had been a single working mother for a long time, and I had become good at all three: great at working, not too bad at being a mother, and as far as being single, there was no other option. I did not have time to date, and another marriage wouldn't survive that cycle of eat, work, sleep, repeat.

As I was lying there next to Dazzle's vomit, it came to me like a dream—how I had come home after another sixteen-hour day, having forgotten to eat my lunch, arriving at my dark house too brain-dead to even turn the lights on. How Dazzle had rubbed against my legs, purring, "Feed me. I'm starving." How I shouted down at him, half-laughing, "You're telling me, brother! At least you get to sleep all day!"

I dug through the pantry and grabbed a fistful of nuts and a fistful of kibbles. "These nuts are so stale and hard, and they taste funny," I thought. But I was too hungry to stop eating them, and Dazzle, too, was chomping away.

Dazzle survived, and I did too, so it could have been worse. Like a heart attack. Or my husband leaving me. Oh, wait. Those had already happened. And I still hadn't stopped being busy at all costs.

Instead of doing laundry, I would just buy more new underwear. I would wake up to exercise at three in the morning. My garbage featured many empty cases of Red Bull. People I really wanted to speak to would leave me a message, and I wouldn't return their calls for weeks. I brought my work to Thanksgiving dinners to avoid wasting time with small talk. I lost my keys at least three times every week. I missed my son's basketball games again and again. I skipped my own yoga classes.

I had become a passenger on a roller coaster that nobody was driving. The cars were just going around and around and around and around, never stopping. It almost killed my cat. It was ruining my couch. Worst of all, it was an old story. The same old, old story.

It was time to fess up and say it out loud:

My name is Peggy, and I'm a Busyness addict.

My editor on this book, Michael, is a recovering addict from substance abuse. He shared with me a basic reality of addiction in his understanding. According to him, addiction is composed of the following few basic facts:

Busyness Is an Addiction

Compulsion	Delusion	Powerlessness
I am powerless over the addiction - I cannot stop.	I lie to myself about the addiction over and over again.	It is ruining my life, and I keep doing it anyway.

Addiction is a bad habit, a self-destructive pattern —exactly what Busyness had become in my life.

BUSYNESS IS AN ADDICTION BECAUSE IT'S A COMPULSION

The realization that being busy was ruining my life actually began more than twenty-five years before I'm writing this book, fifteen years before my heart attack, and a decade before the collapse of my perfect marriage.

The first day I got a glimmer of how bad Busyness was making my life was the day that my first husband, Ray, and I, still very happily married, moved into our dream house.

I was waiting for Ray to get there and for the movers to arrive. I'd taken the day off work, and instead of just letting everyone do their job and directing them, I couldn't wait around. I just had to do something. So I decided to put up some hooks, you know, the kind to hang your towels or bathrobes on. The right way to do that, of course, was to drill holes and screw them in properly. But I had Super Glue and time on my hands, so that was enough.

The next thing I knew, I had one hook on the wall, and my hands were glued together. When the doorbell rang soon after that, I couldn't even turn the doorknob to let the movers in. After some crazy maneuvering worthy of *America's Funniest Home Videos* if there was only someone there to get the shot, I finally managed to get the door open and get the day sort of back on track.

The movers were generous about it, showing a moment of sympathy for my plight before carrying on with their job. Ray, when he got there, was not so polite. He rolled his eyes, as the moving men probably did also. I spent almost the whole day soaking my hands in water, paint thinner, and other compounds until I could finally separate them.

The result of my inability to sit still for even a minute? I was distracted all day trying to pull my hands apart, unable to direct the move, leaving Ray to manage the process all by himself.

What a wonderful first day together in our dream house.

All because I was compelled to be busy doing something instead of focusing on what mattered. It turned what was supposed to be one of the best days of my life into one of the worst.

RECOVERY DOESN'T ALWAYS REQUIRE A ROCK BOTTOM

Addiction is not in the activity itself but in not having the power to say no to it. The behavior controls you instead of you controlling it. And how it controls you is it makes you think it's your free choice. That you are doing this thing because you want to. Because it makes sense. Because it's the right way to do things. Well, I'm sure you've already started to see that it is not.

A compulsion is just a behavioral habit. It's an especially bad habit because it runs itself in specific steps: an initial obsessive thought that triggers anxiety that triggers action intended to relieve discomfort. But the relief is only momentary because the action just causes more problems, and soon, the obsessive thought comes back, and the self-destructive cycle restarts.

Here's an example of how that plays out:

- **Obsessive thought:** I've got so much to do.
- **Anxiety:** If I don't take quick and serious action, I will drown in all this stuff.
- **Compulsion:** I fill my schedule with activities that should hopefully knock stuff off my lists.
- **Temporary relief:** Regardless of being exhausted, confused, and unhappy, at least I got stuff done.

To stop having the compulsion to "use" Busyness, I've had to learn to stop believing the delusion that being busy is going to solve anything.

BUSYNESS IS AN ADDICTION BECAUSE IT'S A DELUSION

After the nut scare with Dazzle, I started looking for a new job. I realized the Medicare industry was an overregulated rat race that I could not slow down and still excel in. Also, it wasn't creative enough.

I landed at Materion, a high-technology manufacturer that had just acquired a number of companies throughout the world. They needed a change management and branding expert. And they chose *me*.

I thought that was the change I needed to fix my life. In the beginning it was fun. I got to travel the world. I was in charge of people around the globe. I felt my work was important to the success of the organization. It was a blast to visit so many new countries for the first time. I got carried away with the excitement of it on so many levels. And I was sure I was managing everything very well.

But after a while, I realized I was using Post-it notes on my nightstand to remind me what time zone I was in. Nothing I did seemed to be enough. The more I produced results, the more they wanted from me. When I noticed the symptoms of exhaustion and strained relationships, I thought I could make it better by working harder. The hamster wheel had started again, only faster.

JUST BECAUSE YOU BELIEVE IT, DOESN'T MEAN IT'S TRUE

One day I made a cunning plan to catch up on my rest during my eighteen-hour flight home from Singapore after a grueling series of meetings. As I settled into my seat, an entire team of sumo wrestlers boarded. Two of them took seats on either side of me. They were so huge they had to lift the armrests to even sit down. So much for relaxing. It was the longest eighteen hours I ever spent, outside childbirth.

When I landed after that flight, I was close to a nervous breakdown. I was living on the edge, where one small slipup would land on me like a catastrophe. I thought I'd solved my problem. But I had not.

Busyness makes us feel better about ourselves because we are filling every moment of our lives with something "important." But it's a delusion. It becomes easy to overlook the fact that I'm throwing away my life minute by minute until a crash or a crisis comes—my husband leaving, my heart failing, my cat vomiting on me.

The Dazzle incident woke me up from the delusion for a few days. But the "lesson" I learned was just another delusion, and soon, the behavior started right up again.

Michael Ashford, coach, speaker, and host of *The Follow-Up Question* podcast, says, "When I think of Busyness, I think of a chicken on a farm pecking continuously for food in the dirt, regardless of if they find any food. Busy people do not set boundaries. I once was a sportswriter for a big newspaper. I was busy all the time because there were so many teams to cover. I got to the point where I couldn't think straight. It was so stressful. It's a bad thing, yet to me, it was a badge of honor."

A badge of honor. Total delusion.

Another delusion is our desire to downplay the impact. "It's not that bad," I told myself again and again. What feels bad in a moment of crisis starts to dissipate the moment it slips into our past. My husband left? But the quiet is nice. I was only in the hospital a few days, right? Once the taste of cat kibble cleared from my tongue, the story became funny.

We pretend we have to be busy. That there is no other choice. That it is the inevitable result of how much we have to get done. But that's not the truth. As with all addiction, Busyness is based on a core delusion—that Busyness is the best solution to the problems we are facing. Actually, Busyness isn't a solution to the problem at all.

The reasons we are busy are justifications, not confessions. We pretend we are busy because we have so much to do, so much to manage—but that's the delusion. The *real* reasons we are actually busy include the following:

- It's a status symbol that makes us feel valued, though it doesn't mean we actually are.
- It makes us look productive and loyal to our job, though, again, it doesn't mean we actually are.

- It helps us overcome our FOMO (fear of missing out)—instead of shopping, we collect experiences, pack our calendars, and fill our social media feeds with our best possible "highlight reel of life," but we're still missing out on what matters most.
- It keeps us filling the time, to satisfy the demands of our 24/7 connected culture.
- It allays our terror of idle moments and allows us to enjoy the abundant options of pointless ways to fill our time.

Perhaps the biggest reason is this: When we keep moving, we don't have to face the tough questions in life.

BUSYNESS IS AN ADDICTION
BECAUSE IT DESTROYS YOUR LIFE

I called Kathy again and again that morning. It wasn't like her to not pick up. We spoke every morning on the way to work. On top of that, she had called me the night before and was really excited about something but didn't have time to share the details. So I was worried that she wasn't answering.

On the other hand, there was probably a good explanation. Kathy was probably the busiest person I ever met. She worked three jobs at once and sometimes four. We would laugh at the fact that she never slept and ate most of her meals in the car. She even kept clothes in her trunk just in case she had to change before she could get home. So she probably just fell asleep or was off doing extra work.

I'd known Kathy for years, and we spoke about everything. She had a tough childhood: her parents were alcoholics, she was hungry all the time, and she had to wear hand-me-down clothes from her church. Kathy worked so hard to make sure her own daughter would never suffer like that. She even admitted to me it was a compulsion she couldn't stop. I can remember telling her one day, "Slow down. Your daughter doesn't need things. She needs you." But how could I expect her to take my advice? I wouldn't have listened to my own input back then.

When the phone was finally picked up, it wasn't Kathy. It was her boss, telling me the sad news that Kathy had died of a heart attack the night before.

I asked the coroner how a forty-year-old dies from a heart attack. He just shook his head, meaning they shouldn't.

For Kathy, being busy was not a logical response to the need for success. It was a fatal disease. Kathy worked herself to death to keep her daughter from suffering, making her daughter miss most of the time they could have spent together and then, finally, leaving her daughter an orphan at nineteen years old.

David Meerman Scott, bestselling author of thirteen books, can relate. I interviewed him while writing this book, and he told me how he once battled with poor health just because he was too busy to make the lifestyle changes required for good health.

Scott said, "When I was super busy, I did not exercise enough, and I did not eat well. Throughout my mid-thirties and my forties, I was sixty-five pounds heavier than I am now and unable to do many of the things I can do now: swimming two miles in an hour, being able to do pull-ups and push-ups. I'm now in my early sixties, and I can do far more. I realize now how much being busy was impacting my health."

THERE IS ONLY ONE SOLUTION: GET INTO RECOVERY

The first time I got into recovery from Busyness was when I left my prestigious job at Benderson Development. This job kept me so busy and high-strung, but it was the epitome of where I thought I needed to go. I was the executive director of an ad agency for one of the largest national developers, and I loved the high-octane environment.

But it was so wrong in so many ways, and I sometimes dreaded going to work. The owner was a young workaholic who expected me to be on call 24/7. Even worse he didn't treat me well and seemed to derive sadistic pleasure in belittling me and pushing me beyond doable limits. But I held on to it.

For a year I kept a letter of resignation in my pocket, bringing it to every meeting. Yet I stayed because I was crushing it. I won national awards for my work. I somehow justified a world of over-the-top Busyness because the accolades were worth the pain.

Until my mom got sick. When she got the diagnosis of pancreatic cancer, I resigned to take care of her. I walked away from something that wasn't healthy, something that was killing me slowly both physically and mentally. Like many addicts, it was an unexpected crisis that threw me into recovery.

Another basic fact about addiction: *You can't stop on your own.* Of course, with more well-known addictions, you don't have to stop on your own. When you are an alcoholic or a drug addict, there are people who have walked a similar path who are keen to help. There are thousands of professionals who are experts in substance abuse and millions of other addicts in recovery. Alcoholics Anonymous, Narcotics Anonymous, and so on offer massive support.

But there is not a Busyness Anonymous. If I wanted to recover from the addiction of Busyness, I would have to create my own recovery program.

The rest of this book is that program. It is a program I have tested on myself and others. And the program works. It has already helped thousands of people turn their lives around by getting off the train of Busyness and embracing a productive but well-rounded life.

The way out of addiction is to start paying attention to the costs—not just the big, crazy, obvious ones but also the ones happening quietly in the background. It requires a full commitment and massive action. As they say in recovery, we won't save our lives by shuffling the deck chairs on the *Titanic*.

When I say, "My name is Peggy, and I am a recovering Busyness addict," I say "am," not "was," because addiction never goes away. All we can really do is the hard work of staying in recovery every day, one day at a time. The temptation of Busyness gets quieter, but it never goes away completely. It's always there, ready for another dance.

So what *does* recovery require? It begins with admitting you have a problem. So the tool below will help you find out if you are, in fact, a Busyness addict like so many of us. And in the next chapter, we'll begin the process of recovery.

BUSY-BUSTING TOOL #2

The Busyness Index

Are you addicted to Busyness? To help clarify this, let's have you do the "Busyness Index."

Answer the following:

	Yes	No
Is multitasking a strategy you use often?	☐	☐
Do you find yourself always handling three or four projects at a time?	☐	☐
Do you keep skipping the time you wanted to spend watching your favorite streaming show or relaxing with a book?	☐	☐
Do you move from one activity to another without finding time to catch your breath?	☐	☐
Do you chase "highs" that Busyness offers, like an adrenaline rush?	☐	☐
Do you find it hard to pause to enjoy the fruits of your success?	☐	☐
Do you eat your meals while doing something else?	☐	☐
Is your to-do list even possible to get to the end of?	☐	☐
Do you book so many appointments that there is no time to get any actual work done?	☐	☐

If your answer is yes to even one of the above questions, then stop and consider whether you are addicted to Busyness. Are you chasing a "Busyness" high that can't be sustained? If it's yes to at least three, there is nothing to consider.

Next, have a look at what Busyness is costing you. Is it ruining your life? Make a list of the damages Busyness is causing. Once you make this list, you will start to see the real cost of your addiction. With addiction, no amount is ever enough. And you always crash eventually. Look into the following:

- Your professional life
- Your family life
- Your personal relationships outside your family
- Your health
- Your sanity

This can and should start to inspire you to get into and stay in recovery. It sure worked for me. When I asked myself this question, I noticed the following:

○○○

- In my professional life, I was wasting time on unimportant things, which was keeping me from doing my best work on the important things.

- In my family life, I was robbing my husband of quality time.

- In my other personal relationships, I was not making time for relationships at all, and the people were feeling neglected and distant!

- In the area of my health, I was missing meals and skipping workouts, and this was leading to more nights of restlessness where I woke up tired in the morning.

- In the area of my sanity, I was literally becoming confused about things I knew, unsure about things I was certain about, and generally taking time each day to have to calm myself down for no reason at all.

I knew I had to do something when I looked at *those* results!

Finally, have a look at the delusion you are experiencing that makes you compelled to be busy all the time.

○○○

	Yes	No
1. Are you trying to avoid something or someone?	☐	☐
2. Do you convince yourself this will only be for a bit of time, it will get better?	☐	☐
3. Feel cranky all the time because you are so focused and one-dimensional?	☐	☐
4. There is no way out except work through it?	☐	☐

CHAPTER 3

THE OPPOSITE OF BUSYNESS

Walter is a dog who lives a few streets over and always sits in his front yard behind an electric fence. I always walk past Walter, just shouting a quick "Hey, Walter!" and then I carry on, totally absorbed in my world and usually with the phone attached to my ear like an intentional accessory. And he sits there looking after me like, "Is that all you got for me?"

But as I was working on dealing with my Busyness addiction, I was more attuned to dealing with things more properly. As such, I decided to take a break from work. I took several deep breaths before stepping off my porch. I walked slowly down the street. I stopped to smell roses—literally. So when I got to Walter, I noticed something I probably would never have noticed before—a butterfly dancing on his long dog nose.

Walter gazed at the butterfly on his nose, frozen in time. It was seconds that felt like days until he finally flipped his nose up to toss the butterfly into the sky. But then it came back and landed on his nose again. After a while, he tossed it into the air, and then, yup, it landed again. This happened again and again and again. It was like they were playing a game with each other.

I was mesmerized and watched this process for I don't know how long. My slow grin turned into a wide smile, and soon, I was laughing wildly, bent over, with tears running down my face.

I couldn't remember the last time I laughed that hard. Ordinarily, I would have missed the whole show, but now I stayed until finally either Walter or the butterfly got tired of it (not sure who made the decision or if they managed to do it together somehow). And I said goodbye to Walter, setting back off on my walk full of lightness and joy.

If I had not intentionally set out to take a break and not be busy that morning, I would have missed that magical moment right in front of *my* nose. The only thing that triggered me to even pause and look and not just wave at Walter was the promise I made to myself when leaving the house to *not* work for thirty minutes. Although in the end, that walk went on for two full hours.

See, the solution to being busy is not to just stop doing anything. That would be not only silly but also impossible. We have way too much to do. The solution is where we put our priorities, choosing what we do with purpose, intention, and clarity.

FOCUS ON YOUR VALUES INSTEAD OF YOUR GOALS
Sally was a single mom working in procurement and juggling a thousand and one things daily. She did what had to be done to provide for her family. Her corporate job sucked the life out of her, but it paid the bills and had decent benefits, so she kept going even though she hated it.

One day they let her go. Sally had thought she would be the one to leave eventually, but instead, the world pushed her out into the cold. While in this state of indecision, she was suddenly let go. It was a bit of a shock since she thought she would be the one to say goodbye to the job rather than her employer making the decision.

It was an answer to a prayer and a curse at the same time. Sally didn't know what to do. She was so incredibly lost. And then a friend invited her to a SheCAN! meeting, and she ended up sitting next to me, Peggy Sullivan. She didn't even know who I was. And she told me she had this dream of having her own business that would give her time to do what mattered to her most—being with her children and helping other people.

So I asked her if those were her values, and after thinking about it for a few minutes, she answered that they truly were: *time* with her children, *fulfillment* from a job that allows her to set her own hours and help others, and the *peace* of mind that comes with being in charge of her own destiny.

And I said, "Why not, Sally? Why can't you live your dream? Why can't you go for what you want? You deserve to be happy and fulfilled."

On the ride home in the middle of winter, she opened her sunroof, blasting music and singing at the top of her lungs. Sally realized it was her chance to open her consulting business and start living the value she cared about most—helping people. Soon, she opened her consulting business. It was just as she'd hoped; she started making good money from it while helping others grow their business.

Recovery from the addiction to Busyness begins
with focusing not on your goals but also
on your values—what you find important.

The opposite of busy is not a lack of activity but rather a conscious choice to prioritize our actions based on our values. It is about finding a balance between doing and being, recognizing that not every task or commitment is equally important or aligned with our core principles.

When we operate from a values-driven perspective, we become more selective in how we invest our time and energy.

Remember I said that time management doesn't solve the Busyness addiction? The best way to recover from the Busyness addiction and go Beyond Busyness is *values management*.

Let's take a moment to reflect on our values. What drives us? What are our fundamental principles and beliefs? Clarifying our values provides a solid foundation upon which to build our actions and decisions. When we align our activities with our values, we find ourselves engaged in meaningful pursuits that bring a sense of purpose and fulfillment.

Why values instead of goals?

1. **Values are enduring.**
    Goals can tend to be short-lived. When you achieve a goal, you tend to succumb to the hedonic treadmill effect: the tendency of humans to return to their pre-existing baseline after a brief period of either upset or bliss. After reaching a goal, we feel happy—for a while. But this increase in emotion is temporary. The goals that last are usually the ones based on values in the first place. Living according to your values brings a daily "adrenaline hit" of ongoing happiness.

2. **When you live according to what you value, you experience joy.**

   When you live in touch with what matters to *you*, your energy improves, you get more endorphins than from exercise, and you radiate this good feeling to everyone around you.

3. **When you live according to what you value, you experience clarity.**

   You align needs and wants. You eliminate the meaningless distractions and focus on what creates the most impact for you and your life.

4. **When you live according to what you value, you feel in control.**

   We can easily get caught in a cycle of feeling controlled by life's challenges: a global pandemic, race riots, gun violence, inflation, recession. Most of what society throws at us is far beyond our control. We end up feeling powerless. When you focus on what you value, you take your power back.

A values-driven approach allows us to distinguish between the urgent, the important, and the trivial things we waste time on. We learn to discern which tasks genuinely contribute to our long-term goals and which are merely distractions or obligations imposed by external pressures. In fact, the most empowering goals are those based on values rather than just achievements.

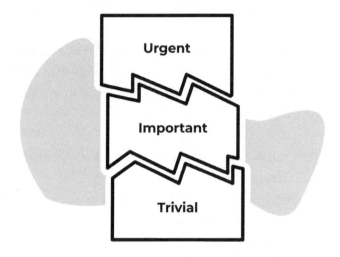

Furthermore, a values-driven mindset helps us establish boundaries and say no when necessary. Often, our Busyness stems from an inability to decline requests or set limits on externally imposed activities that deplete our time and energy.

But when we understand our values and prioritize accordingly, we gain the confidence to decline opportunities that do not align with our core beliefs. This not only reduces our Busyness but also creates space for activities that truly matter to us.

In addition, embracing a values-driven approach fosters a greater sense of presence and mindfulness in our actions. When we are constantly rushing from one task to another, our attention becomes fragmented, and we lose touch with the present moment. By consciously choosing to engage in activities that resonate with our values, we become more fully present and immersed in what we are doing. This enhances our overall experience and allows us to savor the richness of each moment.

VALUES MANAGEMENT PAYS INTEREST— DO WHAT MATTERS

Ashley Menzies Babatunde is an attorney, storyteller, and host of the podcast *No Straight Path*. I met her at a HubSpot INBOUND conference. To her, success means doing impactful work that is meaningful and fulfilling. She shared with me the moment she realized she had lost her path in life.

I was in an Uber on the way to a work event, and the driver asked me about my hobbies. I was shocked. I've always had the perfect answer for "What do you do for work?" But a hobby? Who has time for that?

At that moment I thought, "Is this my life forever? Shiny on the outside but dull on the inside?" I can't quite remember my response. But I was honest.

We both opened up. He told me he was undocumented. I told him about all the advocacy work I'd done for the DREAM Act. I thought to myself, "Wow. That girl was so passionate." The girl who worked her paralegal job and organized advocacy events in her free time. That girl had free time.

I realized in order to become the woman I want to be, I have to have time for myself. Time to read. Time to pour into my passions outside of work. Time affluence.

Harvard Business School professor Ashley V. Whillans describes "time affluence" as the feeling of having control and feeling like you have enough time on an everyday basis. Her research suggests that those who tend to value time over money are usually happier, more civically engaged, and more likely to pursue activities they are passionate about.

Whillans's book, *Time Smart: How to Reclaim Your Time and Live a Happier Life,* delves into this issue. According to Whillans's research, 80 percent of Americans are time poor. Her four strategies for combating this feeling of being time poor are as follows:

Four Strategies for Combating Time Poverty	
Prioritizing time over money	Setting aside time for leisure
Outsourcing unwanted tasks	Believing leisure time is just as important as working

Each of these strategies could be rephrased as speaking to values:

1. Time is more important than money.
2. Leisure is important enough to make time for.
3. I don't need to do things that are not important; others can do them.
4. Leisure is more important or at least as important as working.

When we live according to our values and focus on activities that align with our principles, we become more selective about how we spend our time, focusing on what truly matters. As a result, we experience a greater sense of time affluence because our days are filled with purposeful pursuits rather than mundane obligations.

In turn, living a values-driven life gives us a sense of fulfillment, contentment, and satisfaction that actually shifts our experience of time itself. We start to perceive time more expansively and feel the true abundance of time rather than the illusion of scarcity that drives our need to be busy in the first place.

This feeling of abundance helps take us into focus and even flow states—complete immersion in the present moment, like I experienced with Walter the dog. Flow experiences heighten our sense of timelessness, and we move through life effortlessly. It is also worth mentioning, as you will read about later, that focus makes us more productive and improves the quality of our efforts.

So is it worth investing a little time in recalibrating yourself to focus on your values? You can probably tell I sure think so.

Values management is like insurance for your personal satisfaction. It makes life worth living. A values-driven life is your yellow brick road, but even better because you don't have to be ambushed by witches, monkeys, or a wizard behind the curtain.

DRIVE YOUR OWN CAR—YOUR VALUES DEFINE WHO YOU ARE

In writing this book, I asked some people I respect about their values and how their values helped shape their choices. Madelyn Blair, PhD, is a resilience consultant, TV show host, speaker, and bestselling author. This is her story:

Early in my career, I was named a division chief at the World Bank. It was my responsibility that the division did its work well. And since I was one of only six women in the bank's leadership at that time, my performance would impact women and their opportunities. In my three years in that position, my division met every business objective set by management, always remained within budget, and had a happy and motivated staff, achieving the ninetieth percentile in the annual attitude survey. On top of that, it grew several times larger because of the need for its services.

I made sure my team knew they were valued. I learned that from my mom, who had been disfigured by an accident at five years old and so had to compensate to make sure people felt comfortable around her by her behavior. So respecting others is one of my core values. And another is authenticity. Respect and authenticity permeate every decision I make, business or personal. I simply will not violate these values.

Then the manager of my World Bank department left his job, and the new director who replaced him was far more aggressive, even insulting. He seemed to enjoy denigrating employees in front of one another, playing them against one another, and making promises he didn't keep. I realized that to succeed in his department, I would have to compromise my values, or at the very least pretend to, which, since that would be inauthentic, would also be impossible for me. It was hard to explain to some people why I had to leave. But it was very easy to explain to myself.

So Madelyn Blair, division chief of World Bank, quit her dream job as soon as it no longer aligned with her values.

Now someone else may have had different values and made a different decision or been driven away by different challenges. Because, of course, values are personal and unique to each of us. Only you can truly unearth and define your own values; no one else can do it for you.

Your life is a complex web of experiences, upbringing, cultural background, education, and personal reflections. These factors have contributed to the formation of your values, the tapestry of beliefs that guide your interactions with the world.

Your journey is unique, so your values are as unique as your fingerprints. Your unique set of encounters and lessons have shaped your worldview. And even if someone else had the exact same experiences in life as you did, their values might be different because in the end, values are a matter of choice. What may hold deep meaning and importance to you might mean nothing to your neighbor. You might value honesty—speaking the truth no matter what—while someone else prioritizes compassion—holding back on the truth to save someone's feelings.

Is one or the other better or more correct? Of course not. And while our society might hold certain values higher than others, it doesn't mean these are necessarily true or correct. They are just held by us as a collective, a cultural agreement.

This book is not talking about cultural values but your own. Often, succumbing to cultural values ahead of my own personal values is exactly what drove me to drown myself in Busyness.

Values can encompass a wide range of areas, including ethics, relationships, career, spirituality, personal growth, and more. And the process of determining our own values is a deeply personal journey. It requires self-reflection, introspection, and active engagement with our thoughts, emotions, and desires. Turning inward and exploring our inner landscape helps us gain a clearer understanding of what truly matters to us.

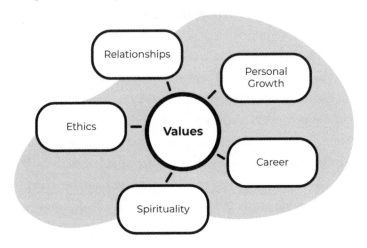

But it also helps to look outside ourselves: What really attracts us in life, if we are honest about it? What, outside ourselves, do we really, truly care about? Society, culture, family, and friends all play a role in shaping our beliefs and worldview. More importantly, how we relate to all this shows us what we value and believe in when we might feel confused.

In short, it takes both self-awareness *and* awareness of how we fit into the world around us to really get clear on our values in a way that will empower us to overcome the addiction to Busyness and stay free of it. It takes hard work and being alert to become and remain congruent with our authentic selves.

And that's why no one else can tell us what our values are. They might as well try to control our thoughts. Our values reveal our essence. Our values are the very core of who we are. And that is, of course, why when we do not live according to our values, we will stay busy no matter how much time we dedicate to doing things and no matter how hard we work.

When we realize that our values must come first and that only we can determine those values, we liberate ourselves from the Busyness cycle. We empower ourselves to unshackle ourselves from doing what doesn't matter. Or at least, when we have to do what doesn't matter, we realize that is what we are doing, and we get it done with full awareness of what is really going on.

Living and acting according to our values and beliefs invites us into a continuous process of self-discovery, growth, and quality of life. Indeed, when we prioritize our values first, we stay present, mindful, and alert—just as I was with Walter. And again, being in the moment means we cannot possibly be "busy" because in the moment there is only what is and nothing else.

LIVING YOUR VALUES MAKES YOU A BADASS

Busy and badass are two ends of the spectrum.
A badass is focused, clear, productive.
They shave away the unnecessary.
They connect with what is truly important to them.

—CARLA JOHNSON, innovation architect,
global keynote speaker, and author of ten books

Saleema Vellani is the CEO of Ripple Impact, the company that helped me fuel the publishing of this book. Her company was struggling to survive because she did not think about her values.

One day I looked through Asana, and I saw my team leaders had a gazillion tasks, and their team members didn't have hardly any! The lower down the totem pole they were, the less they had to do. Our leaders weren't leading; they were just working.

And I was the worst of it. I had traded my visionary self to become a workhorse, dragging my entire company behind me. I was working 5 a.m.–11 p.m. most days, I had gained thirty pounds, and all I was doing was putting out fires and cooling down hot potatoes!

A friend of mine, Tanjina Shapiro (who later became our fractional COO), asked me how my values aligned with the company values. And I realized I had lost track of both! Because I wasn't clear on my values as the founder and leader, I ended up creating a company with values misalignment.

I initially didn't think values were as important as, say, getting the legal and HR departments up and running. But my friend made me realize that values are the foundation for everything, including incorporating values alignment into the hiring process and across the entire company and even choosing clients who align with our values.

She guided me to facilitate values workshops with our senior leadership team, which got us aligned and

also brought us closer together and shifted our mindsets.
I've been through a few lifequakes, and I can't say this
one was better, but it was easier to process when I stayed
focused on values. Coming from values instead of goals
gave me strength. It turned me into a real leader instead
of a Clydesdale pony. Values were my ticket out of the
mess and into success.

Someone in the 1950s invented the word "badass" to refer to bullies and only men. In the late 1960s, it was deappropriated to apply to tough guys who were heroes—Clint Eastwood and Charles Bronson characters—and in 1971, Melvin Van Peebles's blaxploitation character in *Sweet Sweetback's Baadasssss Song.* To be a badass, according to the *Urban Dictionary,* was to be "the epitome of the American male."

But in the past decade or so, the word "badass" has been reappropriated to apply to women. When a man is called a badass today, it is not necessarily a compliment. But for a woman . . . One article[*] lists them on and on: "Beyonce and Malala and Jennifer Lawrence and Nicki Minaj and Ruth Bader Ginsburg and Viola Davis and Amy, both Poehler and Schumer. And also, yes, Charlize Theron."

Today, "badass" conveys strength, confidence, independence, empowerment, and even a bit of a swagger. It no longer connotes a necessary violence or any kind of physicality. There are a lot of ways to understand the word "badass" as it is used today. Badasses overcome challenges, break societal norms and stereotypes, and

---

[*] Megan Garber, "How 'Badass' Became a Feminist Word," *The Atlantic,* November 22, 2015, https://www.theatlantic.com/entertainment/archive/2015/11/how-badass-became-feminist/417096/.

stand tall in the face of adversity. Badasses pursue their passions without apology. Badasses embrace themselves, flaws and all.

But you know who really, most definitely, is not a badass? A person who is stuck in the Busyness addiction. You *have* to go beyond busy to become a badass. You *have* to know and embrace your values.

In fact, the original title of this book was *Go from Busy to Badass*. I even mocked up cover designs. Many people loved the title. But the mainstream media wasn't keen to see the word on their screens, and many large corporations said they wouldn't be able to buy it for their employees or keep it in their libraries.

Still, the fact that so many people, and especially women, today connect with the idea of badassery makes it worth paying attention to as a state they want to reach—one of the core values they want to live by.

If you are being a badass, you cannot be busy. They are mutually exclusive. A badass gets stuff done without experiencing all the negative aspects of Busyness.

Now the challenge, of course, is, if you are a Busyness addict, you'll have lost track of your values or drowned them in false values. The good news is, they're still in there somewhere. And now we're going to begin the process of unearthing them—permanently.

BUSY-BUSTING TOOL #3

Values Rough Draft

Make a list of your top five core values below. Don't think too much about them. Just put down the first ones that come to you.

Core Values

1.
2.
3.
4.
5.

Now we are going to put them into a table and do some further work with them.

First, make some short notes about why they are important.

Second, honestly rate your current state for each value on the list, from 0 to 4, with 0 meaning you are not living it at all and 4 meaning it is at the core of every moment of your existence.

Value	Notes	Rating

Now pick the value you rated currently lowest and come up with five actions you can take to increase that score.

Actions I Can Take

1.
2.
3.
4.
5.

Now take one of the above actions.

I mean right now.

This Very Minute

CHAPTER 4

GO FROM BUSY TO BADASS

My first memory of being a badass is at the age of four. I am standing there, staring fifty feet straight down at the clear water. I'm wearing a swimming cap and goggles, and it seems more like fifty miles.

After my father taught me to swim, he wanted me to learn to dive. And typical of him, he thought it would be cool if my first dive was off a ten-foot board. He thought it would be a good way to overcome my fear of heights.

I didn't even know I was afraid of heights before that. That day, I learned how scary being over fifty feet off the ground can be. (It sure felt like fifty feet.) I didn't see any other little kids climbing that very tall ladder. I climbed the ladder to the top very, very slowly, more and more afraid with every rung.

"You can do it," he whispered from below me. At least it sounded like a whisper; he was soooo far away.

This is not only the highest diving board I'd ever been on; it's also surely the highest thing I had ever seen in my life. And I had never dived into the water even from the pool's edge, even from an inch above it, much less this far.

My fear stood above me like King Kong. It was like being on a mountain in the Swiss Alps. I stood there as long as I possibly could, staring down at the water. It seemed like hours, and it honestly must have been at least a good few minutes because soon, every single one of the people in the lounge chairs around the pool had turned their heads up to stare at me.

Their stares were the only thing keeping me from turning around and climbing back down. That and my worry that climbing down was even more dangerous than jumping.

And then I said to myself, "What's the worst that is going to happen? The water's gonna snap my belly?" That sounded funny, and I giggled at myself, even if not out loud. I told myself to just get it over with. How bad could it be?

I wanted to close my eyes, but I kept them wide open as I stepped off the platform. Falling tickled my body and energized my spirit. It didn't last long enough for me to be afraid anymore. Before I knew it, the adrenaline rush ended in a splash.

When I got out of the pool after the dive, all the people in their lounge chairs were applauding. They were clapping for *me*. That felt amazing! It was a bigger rush than the dive itself. I wanted to do it again right away. So I did. I didn't even bother to towel off.

The second time, I felt far less fear. But the dive still felt awesome. And even though the applause didn't come the second time, I didn't need it as much. I internalized the great feeling of being the only girl my age jumping off that board.

I was far too young then to know what my values really were or to know I was living them. But when I look back, it is clear. I was living *full out*, according to what mattered to me. I was doing hard things, stepping out of my comfort zone, scared but determined. I was living my values, not my fears.

I ended up doing a lot of competitive diving later in life. But that was just the tiniest portion of the real benefit my father's encouragement promoted. What it really did was teach me what it was like to be a badass. It gave me a sense of empowerment I had never felt before. And the elements of being a badass that I learned that day apply across every single part of my life today.

I had discovered the tools needed to overcome my addiction and take control of my life.

The opposite of being busy is not being less busy. The opposite of being busy is getting aligned with your values. This shifts your activity from being about "getting things done" to being about what really matters to you. And in that way, whatever happens, happens. If you don't accomplish as much as you hoped, you have still been doing it inside a way of life that is itself an accomplishment.

In making the journey from goal-seeking to values-living, I have learned that there are four basic "areas of life" you need to focus on. I call these keys to unlocking quality-of-life value clusters. And if you want to live full out, you will need to unpack each one. When you do, you will be well on your way to the fine art of badassery and truly know what it means to feel like a badass. The best feeling ever!

THE SHORTCUT TO BADASS:
THE FOUR CORE VALUE CLUSTERS

Of course, you need to decide on your own what values matter to you. However, in my own journey, certain guiding principles have emerged again and again as the values that make the biggest difference, not only to me but also to those badasses I've interacted with.

These aren't exact values but groups, or clusters, of values, categories of values that have formed the cornerstone of my life. They have helped me forge meaning, build resilience, and anchor myself. They have freed my self-expression and ignited my passions. Though deeply personal to myself and those others I've mentioned, they also seem to resonate universally.

Here they are:

4 Important Categories of Values

Connection　Energy

Growth Mindset　Authenticity

1. CONNECTION

Shortly after my husband, Ray, left, I felt down and depressed. My son, who was only thirteen years old, demanded I get dressed up one

Saturday night and go out with him for date night. (Saturday was always date night with Ray.) He looked a bit awkward that night and kept on pulling up his pants, but they always seemed to drop down again. When it came time to pay, I found out why—he hauled out a big pile of change from his pocket.

He had saved up months of pocket money. A massive pile of it. He paid for dinner. This cheered me up beyond measure. My son was a grade-A badass!

At such a young age, he already wanted to do something that made me feel that Ray's absence didn't matter. The two of us were enough. We started doing really fun things together after that, such as when we went to visit New York City and rode more than two dozen times around Central Park in a horse buggy.

When I finally started dating again, my son would interview my dates to be sure they were good enough. And if he found them lacking, he would put shaving cream in their shoes as his way of letting me know.

Badassery does not come from yourself alone. It comes from *connection* to the people around you. By connection, I mean many things: community, love, family, faith. It also means focus.

Erik Qualman, bestselling author of *Socialnomics*, says that connection is the secret sauce that enables badasses to contribute: "A badass is a rock star. They want to establish a bond, be there when they are needed, and create a relationship—if only for a moment. That's the person I want in my foxhole. Someone I can trust, relate to, and count on when needed."

Connection is like a garden. It can only thrive in a space where there is enough time to water. Bonding and supporting each other is what makes us human.

2. ENERGY

Sheri Sullivan is another epitome of badass. She is one of the most successful women I know. She's a female equity partner for Ernst & Young and has built and grown an international team for the organization in nearly two hundred countries. She oversees more than 4,500 employees around the world. None of that is why I say she is a badass.

With all that on her plate, she remains a nonstop bundle of energy. She is always moving forward, and nothing ever stops her. Give her a problem to solve, and she will figure it out. When confronted with an "either or" situation, she will find a third, more optimal solution. You know that movie *Planes, Trains, and Automobiles*? Well, once when Sheri had to watch her son at a big wrestling tournament in the same week she had to visit an important client on the other side of the country, she managed to do both.

Sheri uses dancing to keep up her positive energy. Her theme song is from Pink: "I'm never gonna *not* dance again!" She'll make sure to dance whenever she's traveling, whether she's in Chicago or China. And it is this commitment to always keeping her energy high that makes Sheri a true badass.

Badasses are energy givers. They walk into a room and light it up. They radiate energy and share it with everybody. Energy is our most precious resource. Many people say time is, but I disagree. You can have all the time in the world, but it's useless without energy. Give me just an hour with a dynamo like Sheri, and we can change the world.

Peak performance is not based on time and money but on energy—not just generating energy but also maintaining it and sharing it with others as an energy *giver*, a net exporter of energy. And also being able to run without much energy from others—being self-sufficient and generous at the same time.

Your heart generates the largest electromagnetic field in your body. It pumps two thousand gallons of blood every single day, enough to fill a water storage tank six feet in diameter and ten feet tall, generating enough energy to power a truck to drive twenty miles. So don't waste all that hard work and raw materials. Use your energy to make a difference.

Energy also touches on self-belief. Nelson Mandela said, "Everything seems impossible until it's done." Every time you accomplish something that seemed impossible until you did it, you are embracing your badassery.

And what does achieving something "impossible" require? It begins with the belief that you can do it, which gives you the courage to go for it. You will never achieve such self-belief while being busy. Busyness always introduces a sense of doubt—can I really keep all these balls in the air?

The key is to understand that being an energy giver does not mean giving away energy we need for ourselves. Financial experts always advise us to pay ourselves first, even if it means we can't pay all our other bills. We should approach our energy the same way. By putting our energy to ourselves first, we create more energy to share with others. When we are busy, we fritter away our energy in a wasteful way, leaving nothing for ourselves to share with the people we love.

Energy is a two-way street. It lights up not only you but also everyone around you. That's why we love being around bundles of energy. It is utterly contagious.

3. GROWTH MINDSET

Dr. Megan Scherer took six years to complete her doctorate at Northeastern University. Candidates are given seven years to finish. She finished with a year to spare. When she walked across the stage in Boston to be hooded, her two young children were in the audience. She wanted them to see that despite what life throws your way, being curious will carry you over the finish line. We are meant to learn and grow. It just makes us better.

Curiosity is a very powerful quality. The more curious you are about a topic, the more likely you are to remember it. When you are open to learning about people, it fosters better relationships. It's why Abraham Maslow placed curiosity at the top of his hierarchy as a form of personal development or "self-actualization."

Badasses color outside the lines. To do that they need to be curious, have a growth mindset, take chances, experiment, and be inspired to look for ways to do things differently. They have a sense of wonder about life.

As Dr. Scherer said, "A badass is not afraid to challenge the norm or assert themselves when something's not right. It's being comfortable with the uncomfortable because that's how you learn."

4. AUTHENTICITY

The call came in the middle of the night. My dad's girlfriend was frantic. He had fallen and couldn't get up. I'd never heard him scream and cry like this before. Breaking his hip at eighty-eight years old was a pretty bad thing. But it wasn't the worst thing that had ever happened to him. Not by a long shot. His family were Holocaust survivors. They left Germany with nothing, not even the ability to speak English. So what was the problem?

At the hospital, Dad answered my question. He had a friend who had a similar fall, and his life just unraveled after that. He wasn't able to do the things he wanted and needed to. Was this going to happen to him?

Well, it did. After the surgery, Dad lost a lot of mobility and had to go to rehab. And because he was so sedentary, the doctors became afraid that pneumonia would set in. The only way to keep this from happening was to drink what he called "the thick stuff." This was medicine that countered his pneumonia.

He hated the thick stuff. A lot. One day they called me to come to the director's office of the rehab facility. I was terrified—another setback? Not exactly. Dad had thrown a glass of the thick stuff at a nurse. My husband, Tom, laughed. But it was not funny. We had to take Dad out of the facility, and less than a week after that, he passed away.

But this is not a sad story. Dad needed to live his life on his terms. Authentic to the dogmas he held dear. Losing his independence and dignity was unbearable. He told me he threw the thick stuff so he could come home. He was not going to shortchange what ended up being the last few weeks of his life. Dad chose to die where and when he wanted. What mattered to him was not life but the quality of his life. Dad died authentically, being true to his beliefs. A total badass.

Authenticity inspires people, gets them engaged, and makes them loyal. Authenticity comes across as confidence, passion, and trustworthiness. Authenticity means sharing your uniqueness, and there's nothing people admire more than uniqueness. It might seem people admire more superficial traits such as wealth, but wealth without authenticity doesn't actually inspire anybody.

At its core, authenticity takes us right back to purpose. When you're authentic, you're always being true. You can admit your insecurities. You can share your strengths with pride. Authenticity means you're loyal to your own personality, values, and spirit, regardless of the pressure that you're under to act otherwise. You own your choices. You speak your truth.

But authenticity does not just mean doing or saying whatever you feel like at the moment. It requires intention and practice. And still, it's easier than the alternative. Being someone else is hard work. Being authentic starts with realizing and aligning intentionally with your core values.

Being intentional about aligning with your values is authentic. And as such, it allows you to connect firmly and without reservation to your purpose and define success for yourself, not according to what anyone else thinks but entirely based on your own heart and spirit. The best person you can ever be is yourself.

COURAGE: THE ROOT OF BADASS

When I was in college, studying graphic design, I got a stomach flu and was out for two weeks. When I got well again, I realized the deadline for this design competition I had eagerly wanted to join was the next day. We were supposed to bring numerous examples of our best work to present to representatives of this international company offering a design scholarship.

I decided to go for it, but there was no way I could catch up with the preparation. So I walked in the door and dug down deep with every ounce of courage I could muster. I told them, "I'm sorry, I have been sick for two weeks. But you don't need to see my work. Instead, you need to know I will work harder than anybody else ever has or will. I will do whatever I can to make the most of this opportunity. I will work hard. But I will also work smart. I was raised by an immigrant who knew how to do both. It is part of my DNA."

I was only partly surprised when I ended up getting the scholarship. I had the courage to take a nontraditional route. Just be brave and take a risk.

Courage is perhaps the single most important trait of badassery. Feelings of bravery and empowerment bring numerous psychological and social benefits: higher self-esteem, greater well-being, better romantic relationships, and enhanced work performance.

Courage helps you ignite your passions. It enables self-confidence and self-respect. It also makes others respect you, of course. It helps build enriching relationships. It fosters happiness, optimism, and resilience, and it kills regret in its tracks. Courage makes you the author of your life, as clearly as I am the author of this book.

Courage to take action is really at the core of everything. Determining the rest of your values starts with having the courage to go after a more meaningful life. Courage allows you to be true to yourself. When you have courage, you don't look to others for approval or surrender to peer pressure.

Courage is about being present in the moment, confident, genuine, and communicating openly. When you are being courageous, you take actions aligned with who you really are. You embrace relationships with people and organizations that allow you to be your truest self. You have honest conversations. You form real bonds.

Courage is a liberating force that empowers us to take a path in life consistent with who we truly are. So recovery from the addiction to Busyness starts with being authentic. Being authentic takes less energy than putting up a front. It helps us perform better. It breeds trust and loyalty. Most of all, it makes it so much easier to distinguish the rest of your values.

Courage is closely related to authenticity. You need to maintain the courage to be authentic when circumstances tempt you to go off the track. And when you are authentic, you end up being satisfied.

Courage also helps you focus and commit. As Carla Johnson said, "I once tried to do multiple careers at once: consulting and speaking. I really yearned to just do speaking and let go of the consulting, but I didn't, and both suffered. Everything got so much better when I focused on speaking. It gave me time and space to be more thoughtful and actually cut down my hours. I slowed down and became so much more aware."

SATISFACTION GUARANTEED

I was approaching my fiftieth birthday and felt like I had so many loose ends in my life. I was sharing this sense of unraveling to my friend Trish and saying I wanted to find some control, do something that made me feel on top of things. She suggested we go running, and then I said, "OK, let's run a marathon!"

I have no idea why I said that, and as soon as I did, I felt a sense of terror. But hey, courage, right? And Trish said, "Look, there's a Rock 'n' Roll Marathon in a few months out in Arizona." We signed up to run in it.

Every few years I like to actively go out and prove to myself and others that I can do something that is nontypical for somebody of my age or experience. But I mean, running twenty-six miles? What was I thinking? It's not like I had been running for years and building up to twenty-six.

To start with, I had to train in Buffalo in the middle of winter in deep snow. When the snow was too deep, I ran around this track near my house that was barely two miles long. This meant I had to run around it twelve times to do a marathon distance.

When we finally ran the marathon, they had bands playing all along the route—rock and roll! We couldn't stop to watch them play, of course, but we could hear them. In the morning it was only forty degrees Fahrenheit, but by the end of the race, it was going to be more than double that. So we went to Goodwill and bought layers and just threw them off in the street. I hoped some people in need might pick them up.

Somewhere on the way, Trish accidentally lost her lucky sunglasses. And she refused to continue the race without them. So we stopped off at a drugstore to get new ones.

How's that for badass? Trish stopped our marathon to get new sunglasses so she could run the race the way she wanted. They were her good luck charm. She could do anything with them. This inspired me even more, so when I hit the wall and my legs felt like literally half a ton, I thought, no *way* am I quitting. And I didn't.

Tom, who would become my second husband, gave us each a dozen roses when we landed back at the airport in Buffalo. And he joked, "What's the big deal? I commute to work every single day as far as you ran." We laughed and felt so special. Pure badass gold.

I wasn't a badass because I ran more than twenty-six miles. I was a badass because I enjoyed it. What started as a joke with a new friend turned out to be one of the greatest experiences of my life.

A badass doesn't just make lemonade out of lemons. A badass looks for lemons so that they can make lemonade. It's not just about taking what the universe gives you and doing your best with it. It's about getting the universe to give you what you *ask for*.

Being a badass is about being unstoppable because it's fun.

All the other qualities of badassery add up to this: a badass is satisfied—or to use an even simpler word: *happy*.

WHAT MAKES A BADASS?

You'll notice something about the qualities I've listed above. None of them can coexist with busy. You can't connect if you're busy. You can't maintain energy if you're busy. You can't grow if you're busy. You can't be authentic if you're busy. And you certainly can't be courageous or truly enjoy your life if you're busy.

As we discussed earlier about being a badass in general, all these elements of what makes a badass also help you see clearly that you have started to go Beyond Busy.

In the last chapter, I quoted *Esquire* magazine in a list of some of the women who are badasses. Here are a few more, both real and fictional:

Olivia Benson—twenty-one seasons of fighting for the underdog on *Law & Order* while raising a child as a single mother.
Arianna Huffington—she has written more than a dozen books, founded a magazine and website, and been named to *Time* magazine's list of the world's 100 most influential people.
Didi Wong—a personal friend and colleague who educates the world about important topics such as human trafficking.

As you can see, there is nothing about what these people *do* that makes them a badass. But all of them embody the four qualities I have listed above more than anything.

Now you will also notice that the more you embody all four of those qualities, the more you truly become a badass and can go Beyond Busy.

And although ideally you do embody all four of those areas, it's better to be strong in two or three than none of them.

If you don't connect, don't maintain your personal energy, have a fixed mindset, and do not embody courage, this is the kind of person you will start to appear as:

- Superficial
- Self-serving
- Arrogant
- Disrespectful
- Hypocritical
- Deceptive
- Taking the easy way out
- Being worried about what other people think

No human being is *born* busy. We become busy. I believe that we are born badasses until it's beaten out of us. So we don't have to learn to become badass. We have to learn to recover our innate badass.

To recover our badass requires intentional action. Cementing our purpose doesn't happen overnight. You have to lay it out bit by bit, like building a railroad. When I ran that marathon, I broke my training into incremental challenges, smaller steps that helped me move forward a little bit every day. I gave myself credit for each milestone. I celebrated every inch of forward motion and got excited about each little triumph. Progress begets progress. Purpose lights us up.

All this needs a system. It needs accountability and support. In the next chapter, I will introduce you to my Busy-Busting System. But first, try this tool out.

BUSY-BUSTING TOOL #4

The First Step from Busy to Badass—Prioritize Your Values

Write the words "Connection," "Energy," "Growth Mindset," and "Authenticity" on a piece of paper in four columns, then write down five other words that come to mind under each—like so:

Connection	Energy	Growth Mindset	Authenticity

These might be other qualities or values, reminders of something you experienced, or the names of friends who have these qualities.

Any words at all you think of are fair game. In fact, make sure to write down the first ones you think of. Don't edit these lists or wait until you've found the right word.

Now think about, or even write about, what these words reveal about yourself and your relationship to each of these four clusters.

The point is to get yourself connected to how these four clusters are playing out in your life.

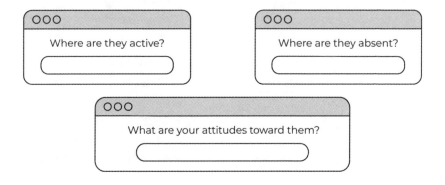

To go Beyond Busy, you need to increase your attention to all four of these areas. And awareness is a great place to begin.

CHAPTER 5

UNLOCKING YOUR VALUES— YOUR VITAL COMPASS

Cathy is a devoted single mother of two children with a full-time job as a corporate executive. When I spoke to her, she had no idea what her values even were. She couldn't leave her family behind to go sit on a mountain and figure it out.

So instead, she started marking out tiny pockets of time for solitude and reflection and jotting in her journal just before the kids woke up or between dropping them at school and arriving at her office. At least once a week, she would take her lunch break in a park near work, taking a walk and staring at the trees.

Soon, she had filled an entire notebook with her ponderings, and she realized that self-reflection alone was not enough. She started to talk about this question with her friends and colleagues, and she soon discovered that they, too, had little idea what their values were.

Finally, Cathy decided what her values were: compassion, growth, community, empowerment. She found herself cutting out activities that didn't fit with them and taking on things that did. These include things she never imagined she would do, such as volunteering at a community organization that helped small businesses connect to customers in their neighborhood. And then she realized her job only offered her money.

She went to her boss and asked if it was possible to shift her responsibilities to focus more on the values she believed in. Her company did not have a coaching program or a community outreach program, but her boss did agree they could use both.

So Cathy reinvented herself as the leader of both these initiatives over the next two years.

VALUES ARE NOT COOKIES, SO DON'T MAKE THEM WITH COOKIE CUTTERS

Some years after my first husband left me, I decided I was never going to find a new partner if I left it to chance. As a single working mother, I wasn't getting out much.

So I joined dating sites, and every night after work, I spent time interviewing men. I set aside a couple of hours every Saturday to meet three men whom I had first met online. I would go to a coffee shop to meet man number one. After completing interview number one, I would drive around the block a few times as a form of palate cleansing, then arrive back at the very same coffee shop for man/interview number two.

And yes, I would do the same for interview number three. I guess, in addition to giving myself a jump start with men two and three, I was also making it look a bit less weird than it would if they showed up early, and I was already there. It made it feel like more of an adventure as well.

My friends thought this was a really strange way to look for a new partner. And I guess it was. But it worked! Because that was how I met my second husband.

None of these interviews were even long enough to call dates. They were more like applications for a date. And looking back, I realize now that the questions I was looking to answer in those meetings were, "What values does this man embody?" and "Is he authentic about them?"

I believe people overdo romance. What matters is compatibility. And compatibility ultimately comes down to values. Get out your notebook and jot down this sage advice: values determine compatibility. They say money and religion are the biggest stops to any relationship. And in a way they are. But it's because of the values that are behind them. If your religious and financial values fit, you're off to a great start, even if you are from different religious backgrounds and earn radically different amounts of money.

A total of 96 percent of people in my Busyness survey said that they rate values as critical to their happiness. Three-quarters of them said they know their values, which seemed like good news until we had a closer look and realized that most people listed the *same* values as everyone else: trust, honesty, respect, integrity.

These are very nice values. But for everybody?

In workshops I do on unlocking your values, I get a similar response. People google "values" and then pick from the top ten list because those are the values that a good person has. Just the same way that more than half of companies surveyed say "integrity" is one of their top five values. Yet most can't even define what they mean by integrity.

Your values are as unique as your fingerprints. Unlike your fingerprints, though, you choose your values. You are a unique collection of your experiences, likes and dislikes, and innate abilities. Your values are your true north. Your values—to extend that metaphor—help your compass know where to point you toward.

Values are deeply personal and subjective. They are influenced by our upbringing, experiences, culture, and beliefs. While external influences may shape our initial understanding of values, ultimately, we must embark on an individual journey to determine our own unique set of values.

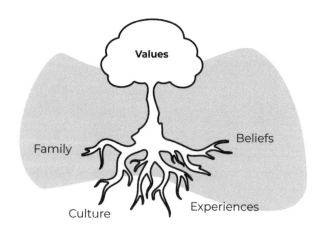

Your values reflect the past, of course—a one-of-a-kind collection of your experiences, likes and dislikes, and abilities. But your values also create your future. They are your road map that keeps you going.

Cathy didn't figure out her values by looking through a list, and neither will you. She embraced small moments of solitude to engage in introspection that allowed her to mine her values from her life just like a gold panner finds flakes in the river that eventually add up to a sizable nugget. And that is how you will do it.

Determining our values is a deeply personal process that requires the willingness to explore our innermost aspirations. You cannot copy them from the internet. You can't just circle them on a list.

So how do you determine your values? You can start by making a list off the top of your head like I asked you to do in the previous chapter.

You can also make a list of what you do each day. Literally, keep track of your schedule. The simplest way to distinguish your values that are already in place is to look at how you behave. Ask yourself for each activity, "Does this activity really connect to what I care about, what means something to me?"

You don't have to worry that this might not be accurate; you will know if you are doing something that means something to you and fulfills your inner spirit. And you will also feel conflict when it doesn't.

And once you do, ask yourself this simple question: what values are behind this feeling of authenticity and connection? Make a list of as many words that come to you as you can think of. If you like, you can even look up synonyms of the words you think of on the internet if that might help you come up with a more diverse list.

It's great to make a thorough list that is as long as you need it to be. From there you can cluster your values into ones that seem connected or similar. Ideally, you want to cut this list down to no more than four or five. And of course, a little tip or trick, you might see if they cluster into the areas I talked about in the previous chapter. In my work with dozens of women, including myself, I have found that they usually do.

4 Important Categories of Values

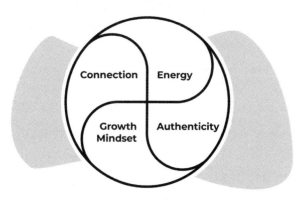

YOU CHANGE—AND SO DO YOUR VALUES

When I was fourteen years old, all I wanted was to become a Sweet Home Senior High Varsity cheerleader. Hundreds wanted to get in, but only the best twelve would make it. That's a 4 percent chance. Best of luck.

The tryouts were in April, but most people spent the whole year before that practicing. It was not just about mastering the craft of cheerleading itself. They assessed the "total package": looks, personality, performance, reputation. The scorecard marked every little detail, and this was an open book, so your scores affected more than just getting on the squad. Doing well was the shortest route to popularity and prestige and all the best parties. In high school, this was what I truly wanted.

Fifty years later, being popular does not motivate me at all. I still value community but in a completely different way.

The point is, not only can you not live other people's values; you also can't live the same values forever. Why would you want to? Your childhood desires are probably not the same for you today. Did you perhaps want to grow up to be a professional athlete, a ballet dancer, or a rock star? What values were behind that?

It's not just since childhood that my values have changed. To overcome my addiction to Busyness, I had to radically shift my values. During my overachieving, hustle approach to life, I valued achievement, perfection, and financial security. Family and service to others were important to me, but they were clearly not at the top of the list.

Although values are like fingerprints, they also aren't because they don't stay the same throughout your life. They shift and change as you have different experiences. So we need to embrace growth.

As we move through life, our values evolve and transform. Embracing personal growth means allowing ourselves to adapt and change as we gain new insights and experiences. What we valued in our earlier years may not align with our present beliefs and priorities. Our values adapt as we gain wisdom, learn from our experiences, and broaden our perspectives.

Therefore, it is essential to periodically reassess and redefine our values to ensure they align with our current understanding of ourselves and the world around us. It requires openness to learning, self-reflection, and a willingness to reassess. So when you wake up one day and realize that circumstances have shifted what you believe in, there's no need to be upset or surprised.

DON'T EAT YESTERDAY'S COOKIES!

Here's what Ashley Menzies Babatunde has to say on this point:

> As a millennial who grew up in an era where we were told we could have it all, I worked towards achieving it. I was influenced by the lean-in era. The girl boss era. Although this ethos was often pushed by privileged white women, I bought into it.
>
> As a black woman afforded a lot of privilege due to my education, I thought I could be a girl boss too. To a certain extent, I became one. Or at least I was on my way. I have worked at prestigious law firms since graduating from college. I'd pull late nights studying in law school and as a summer associate and post it on my IG. I wanted to give my boss vibes.
>
> I was that girl that bought into hustle culture, grind culture, rest-when-you-die culture. I know many of us did. Although I wanted more work-life balance, I didn't know how to achieve it and still succeed. To remain fulfilled, I took on pro bono projects and extracurricular activities.
>
> I also didn't skip out on family time because it was and still is important to me. So basically, I didn't sleep. I was moving through the world exhausted. And I realized that this lifestyle no longer felt successful to me. So I needed to make a change. I needed to redefine success for me.
>
> I realized that having time for myself to reflect, read, and just be has led to more fulfillment and

happiness in my life. When I reflect on my journey, the times where I felt most at peace, happy, and energized were times where I've had time for myself. Times where I actually achieved work-life balance. I can only point to two periods of my life where I've felt like this.

One of them is right now because I have more control over my schedule. And the first time was in the latter half of 2021. I had gone on a reduced schedule earlier that year to give myself time to grieve after my mom passed away.

And in the last six months of the year, I found my rhythm. I was working on some great cases with people I enjoyed working with while also having time for myself, family, and fun. No real commitments outside of work. I could just be. When I have personal time, I can focus on my health and well-being. I can read books. I can actually be an interesting person.

HOW TO DETERMINE YOUR VALUES
AND WHAT TO DO WITH THEM

Here are some basic ways to determine your values:

How To Determine Your Values and What to Do With Them		
Engage in Self-Reflection and Introspection	Identify Peak Experiences	Look for Patterns and Isolate Guiding Principles
Get Authentic	Discuss	Experiment
Clarify Priorities	Get Present	Be Grateful

1. **Engage in Self-Reflection and Introspection.** Taking the time to contemplate your desires, beliefs, and passions can help you identify what truly matters. Journaling, meditation, or engaging in meaningful conversations with trusted individuals can facilitate this process of self-discovery.

2. **Identify Peak Experiences.** Reflect on moments in your life when you felt most alive, fulfilled, or aligned. This could be as extreme as when you were on top of a mountain or as simple as when you saw your baby being born. Either way, these experiences are almost always connected to values that matter to you.

3. **Look for Patterns and Isolate Guiding Principles.** When you analyze your daily life and see what

patterns of behavior emerge, you can then use these patterns as guiding lights, providing direction and clarity to understanding your values. For example, looking at my life recently, I noticed that I was tending to avoid doing the harder things on my to-do list. When I realized that, it became much easier to do them. On the other hand, you might notice that there are no stable patterns—this might show you that you are not living according to consistent values at all, and perhaps you need to do more values work to get things stable.

4. **Get Authentic.** Of course. Peel back the layers of societal expectations and norms that may have influenced you, question assumptions, examine your motives, and embrace your vulnerabilities. Say the controversial thing you know is right to say. Challenge your boss when he is off base. You will often find that what you were most afraid of doing, when it's authentic, will lead to surprising rewards.

5. **Discuss.** Thinking can be useful. But it can also lead to *over*thinking. Get out of your head. Talk to people who know you, and find out what they think your values are. Tell them what you think your values are and see if they agree with you. Other people know you better than you do, according to many studies.

6. **Experiment.** Determining your values, if you are not clear about them, requires experimentation, trying out different values as if you were trying on clothes, and then reflecting on this. Don't buy on an impulse. Take

your time to practice different approaches and find out
which suit you.

7. **Clarify Priorities.** Many people get confused trying
   to figure out which values matter most. One minute
   it seems like it's compassion, the next it's empowerment. Prioritize your values on a list, but be ready to
   be flexible as well (see below).

8. **Get Present.** Living according to values requires mindfulness. Although we tend to maintain our core values
   over long periods, the exact hierarchy of which matters most at any given moment changes from context
   to context. We need to be willing to be flexible and
   attuned to the present moment.

9. **Be Grateful.** Be grateful for the values you have and hold
   to. Be grateful for the values you've forgotten about. Be
   grateful that you get to practice living according to your
   values. Be grateful for the times you fall short. You can
   even try being grateful for your Busyness. Gratitude for
   anything at all clears the mind of unnecessary noise and
   helps you clearly see what matters.

Once you have determined your values, here are some basic
things to do with them:

○○○

What to Do Next

Integration	Setting Goals and Priorities	Making Values-Based Decisions
Challenging Societal Norms	Setting Boundaries	Cultivating Accountability and Reflection
Surrounding Ourselves with Supportive Communities		

Integration. Identifying our values is only the first step. Living in alignment with them requires integrating them into our daily lives. This involves making conscious choices that reflect our values and avoiding actions that contradict them. By aligning our thoughts, words, and behaviors with our values, we create a sense of integrity and authenticity in our lives.

Setting Goals and Priorities. Values provide a foundation for setting meaningful goals and priorities. When our goals align with our values, they become more meaningful and fulfilling. By setting clear intentions and aligning our actions with our values, we can work toward goals that bring us a sense of purpose and satisfaction.

Making Values-Based Decisions. Our values can serve as a compass in decision-making, helping us navigate through life's choices. When faced with dilemmas or difficult decisions, we can refer back to our values to guide us. By consciously aligning our choices with our values, we create a sense of coherence and harmony in our lives.

Challenging Societal Norms. As much as it requires challenging norms to figure out your values, it requires even more courage in challenging norms to actually live them. By consciously choosing to live according to our values, we challenge the societal narrative that Busyness is the only path to achievement. We prioritize our well-being and focus on what truly matters to us, leading to a healthier relationship with time.

Setting Boundaries. Living in alignment with our values empowers us to set boundaries, particularly prioritizing self-care—putting ourself first without being selfish. We learn to say no to nonessential commitments and create space for rest, rejuvenation, and reflection. This intentional approach to time management allows us to recharge, maintain balance, and avoid falling into the trap of Busyness.

Cultivating Accountability and Reflection. Living by our values requires ongoing self-reflection and accountability. Regularly assessing our actions and their alignment with our values allows us to course-correct and make adjustments when necessary. This practice fosters personal growth, ensuring that our actions are in line with our evolving values.

Surrounding Ourselves with Supportive Communities.
Living in alignment with our values can be easier when
we surround ourselves with supportive communities.
Being in the company of like-minded individuals who
share similar values can provide encouragement, inspiration, and a sense of belonging. These communities can
help us stay accountable and reinforce our commitment
to living authentically.

BUSY-BUSTING TOOL #5

The Next Step Toward Badass-Take Value-Driven Action

From the list of values you made in the last chapter, choose one from each cluster and write them in the table below.

Then come up with one action you can take for each of the four values. Put down the date you will take the action. Then take the action.

Values Action Tool

Value	Action	By When
Connection		
Energy		
Growth Mindset		
Authenticity		

Here are some examples of actions I put down on my own Values Action Tool:

Connection

- Add value to every interaction today.

- Give randomly to a person I meet on the street.

- Meet a new person today.

Growth Mindset

- Add a new word to my vocabulary today.

- Go to dinner alone and invite a stranger to eat at my table.

- Try a type of sport I never did before.

Energy

- Have fun.

- Intentionally explore my inner child.

- Do my Sensate meditation.

Authenticity

- Make a list of the people who no longer fit my life. Let them go.

- Give away ten items in my house I no longer need.

- Stay in tonight instead of indulging my FOMO.

CHAPTER 6

THE BUSY-BUSTING PROCESS

The W. E. B. Du Bois Library at the University of Massachusetts was designed to be the tallest library in the United States. It stood 28 stories, more than 250 feet tall. But a few years after it opened, the building had to be closed for some months because pieces of the brick started falling off.

Some experts claimed the reason for this major architectural fail was that the architect had forgotten to factor in the weight of the books stored inside. This accusation has since been proven a myth. It was actually the result of shoddy construction materials and building too fast.

But the story, when I heard it, became a metaphor I've been fascinated with since. There are few works of art more carefully planned than a building. Imagine if an architect forgot to calculate the impact of two-dozen-plus floors of books in a purpose-built library. That would be crazy, right?

We don't build a building without blueprints. We don't try to launch a business without a business plan. When we have a guide or instruction book, we find it easier to complete almost any challenging task. Having detailed information telling us how something should be done takes away the guesswork, difficulty, and stress out of it. And if that process has been tested and worked hundreds or thousands of times, we can have confidence the process will work for us as well.

A strong, effective process is intentional. It doesn't happen by accident. There is a purpose for each and every step. Missing a step can be disastrous.

A GOAL WITHOUT A PLAN IS JUST A WISH

When I cooked my first turkey, I didn't bother to read the instructions that came with the bird. Nor did I use one of my cookbooks. How hard could it be? Clean the bird, season the bird, and cook the bird. This is not rocket science.

I pulled the turkey out of the oven when it looked done. I cut into it to be sure it was thoroughly cooked. My very first turkey was golden brown and smelled delicious. I was filled with a sense of pride. I grabbed a sharp carving knife and brought it to the table. All twelve of my guests were hungry, so we started to cut the bird up. All eyes were on me.

But when I began to carve, I saw this white paper that had turkey parts inside. I didn't know a turkey came with the giblets wrapped inside. When my guests saw my rookie mistake, no one would eat the turkey. They thought it was unsafe to eat. I spent all day basting and preparing a Thanksgiving dinner where no one would eat the main course. It is comical now, but it sure wasn't then. My dad, my biggest fan, left early so he could go home and eat dinner.

TO GO BEYOND BUSY, YOU NEED A PROCESS

I tried to wing cooking a Thanksgiving turkey. It did not work out. Similarly, I experimented with many strategies to mitigate my compulsion to be busy, but I always got back to where I started. Looking back over those years, I realized I didn't have a deliberate process. If I wanted to escape the Busyness trap, I needed to be more purposeful. As we all tend to learn the hard way, "a goal without a plan is just a wish."

Busyness comes from lack of intention and prioritization. We just start doing things to keep up with the goals that we take on or that get thrown at us. Soon, we have such massive to-do lists we just keep going to try to winnow them down.

You know that old saying, failing to plan is planning to fail. We end up doing so many things that don't align with our values, low-value Busyness things. Things that waste our precious time, energy, and resources. This is how we end up stuck in that endless loop, that hamster wheel that keeps us working really hard, but we don't seem to get anywhere. A hamster doesn't know any better.

The rest of this book will teach you a process that will help you avoid the Busy Trap and find your awesomeness. I call it the three-step Busy-Busting Process. I learned this process mainly by accident, by trial and error over many years. Thousands of individuals have used it with great results. It will work for you as well. We will go over this step by step in the next chapters.

The prize you get when you use this process is improved satisfaction: the sweet spot Beyond Busyness. This is a place where peak performance, wellness, and happiness collide without you having to sacrifice one for the other. Your "sweet spot" is something like your very own golden mean. It's about doing, or not doing, that which in any particular situation is optimal for you.

Find Your Sweet Spot: Beyond Busyness

Without Sacrificing One for the Other

Time poverty is real. Feeling overwhelmed and frustrated is real. Going round and round on the hamster wheel is real. But there is a way out, and you will have to put in the work. You need to know that going in. You will *not* be passive in the Busy-Busting Process. You have to do the work. There are no shortcuts. You may even sweat.

If you follow the three-step Busy-Busting Process, you will develop new habits and a new mindset. You will feel renewed. This process creates a space for possibility in everything.

The chart that follows outlines the Busy-Busting Process. While these steps are most effective when you approach them step by step, they are also modular, meaning you can do them individually as well.

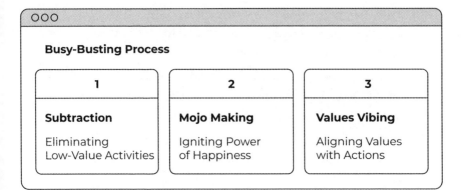

STEP ONE:
SUBTRACTION—ELIMINATING LOW-VALUE ACTIVITIES

Forty years ago, I took a job as an ice cream scooper during my first year in university. I wasn't really keen on hairnets and sticky elbows, but it allowed me to go to classes in the morning, work for a few hours, then study at night. We offered twenty-six flavors of ice cream, and there were two sets of labels identifying each flavor: one on the bottom of the container and one on the top of the lid.

But since we had to place the ice cream in the freezer "topless" for easy scooping, it could get confusing. Strawberry looked like raspberry, cherry, and cinnamon; coffee looked like chocolate; and so on.

To solve this, I created a cheat sheet. For a day it worked like a charm. But when I got there the next day, someone had moved the tubs around. Not that it mattered because they had also thrown away the cheat sheet like yesterday's newspaper. It was a hot day, and lots of people came in for ice cream. I had to keep taking the tubs out to turn them upside down and read the label.

It was a valuable lesson in why we need to avoid LVA: *low-value activity.*

Another example—when I worked for Materion, one of the world's largest suppliers of specialty metals, I had to strip all the metal I was wearing to be able to go into the factory. The line was long, and it took me even longer to take off my belt, wedding ring, watch, cell phone, jacket with zipper, underwire bra, and put them all on again.

Every day I would have to go through metal detectors to get to the plant for daily meetings. This was a negative side effect of working for Materion. No one ever actually stole from the company, but if they did, the cost would have been epic, so they had to take precautions. I wasted so much time waiting in line at the metal detector.

Sometimes I would have to go back into the plant four times in a day, even though I was the director of marketing, and the meetings were largely around operations. These meetings literally took hours and were seldom important to perform my responsibilities.

So it was at this job that I learned how many, if not most, meetings are massive time wasters that turn us into Busyness addicts even against our better judgments.

But meetings are not the only LVAs. Here are a few more:

- "Hey, have you got a minute?"
- Checking your email or chat rooms every hour
- Multitasking since we lose at least half an hour every time we shift our focus to a new activity

- Failing to delegate things you do not need to do yourself

You can fill in the blanks with any others you have suffered through.

Our society has encouraged us to embrace such time wasters. We go on automatic to follow the processes we were trained in, and we stop distinguishing between the worthwhile and the worthless.

We are conditioned to believe more is better. But in life subtraction can be a remarkably effective approach. By removing things we create clarity and focus. What sticks with me most about the concept is the simple pragmatism and prescriptive nature of the word itself—subtraction. How much more direct can you get than to say you need to subtract something? But determining what to subtract and how is the hard part.

We spend our days trying to manage everything in a productive fashion, but we still end up in a state of time poverty. No one sets out to commit what I call "unintentional self-sabotage"—not having time for what's important but it still happens. The only way to prevent it is to understand the different behaviors or root causes that create it. The next chapter gets into the specifics of how you can create more time for what's important.

What's important here is to understand how subtraction creates a space where you have more time, energy, and resources to focus.

Think about your day and all the things you do like a robot, without thinking. How many of those activities produce great value? When we identify and eliminate low-value activities, we free up time and energy for what's important. That's why I call these LVAs "busy traps." And that is why eradicating them is the first step in the Busy-Busting Process.

STEP TWO:
MOJO MAKING—MAKING IT IS BETTER THAN FAKING IT

The *Merriam-Webster Dictionary* defines "mojo" as a magic charm, talisman, or spell. Mojo is like happiness plus—a superpower that allows you to make personal magic.

Mojo Making is the intentional act of creating repeatable happiness rituals. The idea is to schedule them into your day to improve your mood and energy. It should also be noted that doing things that make you happy is also a strategy the medical industry uses when trying to replace the dopamine that comes from addiction.

Feeling good ignites your personal energy. It makes you not only happy but also more efficient and effective. When we have positive energy, there is so much possibility. Mojo Making increases productivity. When you are in a good mood, you are more productive.

Mojo Making promotes better health behavior and choices, enhances immune functions, increases life expectancy, and much more. The benefits of Mojo Making are endless.

Most of us rely on others to bring out our Mojo—friends, family, colleagues, or even our pets. They transform you from a stiff upper-lipper to a happy-go-lucky, fun individual who relaxes, laughs out loud, and enjoys life. Studies show that when a happy person enters a room, everyone's mood improves 87 percent. That is mind-blowing.

For me, the biggest Mojo Maker in my life is my cat. Not Dazzle, whose food I ate, but my current fur baby, Oliver. I know everyone says this about their pets, but Oliver is the cutest cat ever. No matter what mood I'm in, spending time with Oliver recalibrates me in a positive way. So I make it a point to spend quality time with him every day.

Just last night when I was tired from a long week, Oliver crawled on my chest, wrapped his furry paws around my shoulder, and purred wholeheartedly for what seemed like a very long time. It was like he was saying, "Mommy, I love you," and what is more wonderful than being loved?

You might find this funny, but I love to take Oliver out for walks in the fresh air. He starts out sitting in his stroller, and at the end of the walk, I take him out to walk alongside me like a dog. I take a special wicked pleasure in the freaked-out faces of strangers on the street when they realize it's not a baby in the stroller but a cat. Pure comedic gold.

But these walks with Oliver are also just a trigger to help me ignite my Mojo—in reality I could just do it myself without even leaving my seat. We have it in our power to generate our own happiness. It's great to surround ourselves with Mojo Makers. But it's even better to be one.

I've found that there are three kinds of people in this world, in relation to Mojo Making.

Mojo Makers	Energy Zappers	Middle-Roaders
These are the people who walk into a room and light it up, people you love to spend time with because they are inspirational.	Gloom-and-doomers who complain most of the time and find fault with everything, including themselves.	These people think - "Life is okay, but not great." They see the importance of happiness and want to get there, want to put time into their personal development, and so on—but they just don't have time for it because they are too BUSY.

Which one are you? The great thing is you get to choose. Every single day you choose again. Of course, you want to be a Mojo Maker, bringing happiness to everyone around you.

Happiness has positive effects on our well-being, longevity, creativity, and coping skills. It helps us reach our goals and increases our productivity. It promotes altruism. Happy people contribute to the creation of a peaceful and harmonious world. Being happy leads to a stronger immune system and heart, greater resilience, less risk of cardiovascular disease, and quicker recovery times from illness. It can also make you popular because people like being around happy people.

Unfortunately, the vast majority of people are Middle-Roaders. That's because we are all too busy to take the time for Mojo Making. Leaving things to fate doesn't make the odds very good. That's why our happiness survey shows that only 5 percent are consistently happy. We view happiness as a result of our circumstances, a thing, a destination in the future but definitely not possible now.

But hey, Middle-Roading is still better than Energy Zapping.

Mojo Making doesn't cost a lot and isn't difficult. It comes entirely from within. You are never too busy to be happy because it actually takes no time at all. What it takes is intention and a Mojo Making attitude.

In chapter 8 I will show you exactly how to be a Mojo Maker all the time. It involves these key steps:

- Determine your nonnegotiables.
- Make self-care a priority.
- Create happiness rituals.

STEP THREE: VALUES VIBING—UNLOCKING A MORE MEANINGFUL LIFE

One of my dear friends, Paula Dobozin, went on a yoga retreat to Costa Rica with me a few years back. You know Murphy's Law, anything that can go wrong will? Well, this was Murphy's voyage for sure.

Paula carefully selected a special outfit for every day of the trip in advance. But when we landed, Paula's luggage did not arrive. The airport staff could not even track it. So Paula ended up in paradise with just one pair of underwear, which she had on while traveling. We didn't get her luggage until the fifth day of the weeklong trip. And an hour later, the bathroom clogged up and flooded, all over the suitcase.

Most people would have thrown a tantrum or shut down. But Paula was determined to enjoy the trip. What helped her stay positive was she knew her values very well. She told me one night during what we named "the Betsy Ross incident." You know, the woman who sewed the American flag before we invented machines to do so.

Paula was sitting next to me as I was darning her underwear so she could wear them again the next day. She said,

> *Friendship, positivity, and well-being are what matter most to me, Peggy. You are my friend, and I am not going to ruin our trip. I'm here to build memories with you. It's about connecting on a deeper level to you, my yoga community, and myself. Connection is everything. I am learning about yoga practice. I have been curious about the Baptiste method, and now I know how to practice it. A new tool in my tool belt to improve my physical and mental energy.*

Paula was practicing Values Vibing, although I didn't know it then. She aligned what was important to her with how she spent her time. She was happy and fulfilled. Of course.

Watching Paula be so wildly happy made me think about what values contribute most to living a well-lived life. If I could figure that out, it would be the third and final step of the Busy-Busting Process.

That is why I have surveyed thousands of people in workshops to understand what core values result in all-out joy and quality of life. The research was clear.

There are four core value clusters that contribute the most to happiness. Guess what they are. Yup. Connection, growth mindset, energy, and authenticity.

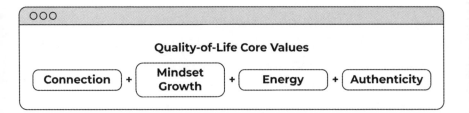

LIVING IT—SETTING YOURSELF UP FOR SUCCESS

I love eating breakfast but hate to make it while still in my morning funk. It means getting up early and putting in work to prepare the food while I'm still half asleep. But when I don't eat breakfast, I end up with low energy all morning.

To deal with this, I found a simple solution: overnight oats. They come in individual packets in really yummy flavors. My favorite flavor is cinnamon roll. It's like eating dessert for breakfast except it is filled with good stuff such as macronutrients.

I make this treat just before I go to bed. It does take some effort but not much. Get the bowl. Open the packet. Add in the milk. And stir. About a ninety-second effort even when I'm really tired. I bring them when I travel, along with bamboo spoons. It became a habit because eating healthy and having good energy are core values. Low energy in the morning is no longer a problem.

There are many theories about what it takes to make a new habit or break an old one. Some people say it takes three weeks; others say it takes three months. What everyone can agree on, however, is that you have to be consistent. You have to take action every day and follow through on what you have set out to accomplish.

New Year's resolutions will never go out of fashion. People love setting goals at the beginning of each year, intending to have them steadily ticked off and completed by the end of the year. While this is nice enough, a report from researchers at the University of Scranton has revealed that 92 percent of New Year's resolutions are broken in the first month.

This shows how important it is to have structures for being accountable for the three busy-busting steps. Accountability makes your values actionable, and actioned, not just pictures on your vision board that you never live up to.

Values are more important than goals. And I'm not the only one who thinks so. Carolyn Gitlin points out,

> *Values drive every good decision I make. I am going out of town, out of the country at the end of the week, but my daughter is struggling, so I decided even though I am busy, she is important. My family is first, so I will drop everything. It doesn't bother me doing the right thing.* Values keep you focused on doing the right things. *My daughter needs me, so I'm going to say "family first" and have to put aside some really important meetings. I think sometimes putting your values ahead of what you want to accomplish is just the right thing to do.*

We all aspire to be happy, healthy, and successful. But what is the recipe to achieve this? For me, the process that works repeatedly is knowing what I value and aligning everything in my life with those values. What do you value? Do you know the core ideals that are most meaningful in your life? Can you actually sit down and articulate them? Many people cannot, and then they wonder why life comes up short.

Taking the time to think about and articulate what you value is a fundamental step toward happiness. You can and should use the four categories (connection, energy, growth mindset, and authenticity) in doing so. Thousands of people I have worked with have used this model to simplify the process for themselves. You can do the same.

You need to know what drives and nourishes you. If you consistently fail to have these things in your life, you will feel unsatisfied. After making your values list, commit to five minutes each day at the end of the day to look back and check if you have lived your values. There is no magic without maintenance. After I made my "What I value most" list and started to measure it daily, things changed.

BUSY-BUSTING TOOL #6

Eliminate Time Wasters

Over the past few weeks, did you have a feeling on some days of not accomplishing what was important to you?

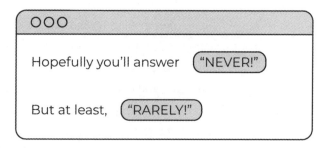

If instead you find yourself saying "MUCH OF THE TIME" or "MOST OF THE TIME" or, worst of all, "ALWAYS!" then it's time to take a small step toward eliminating time wasters.

First, make a list of what *low-value* things kept you from getting to what you really wanted to do.

Then make a list of what you will do differently.

You can use the following table.

Low-Value Things That Stopped Me	What I Will Do Differently

Here is an example from my own life. Feel free to steal any you like.

Low-Value Things That Stopped Me	What I Will Do Differently
Meetings without a purpose or agenda	Make sure all meetings are well thought through
Did too many tasks I should have delegated	Practice delegating, even where it might go wrong
Not taking enough breaks to recharge	Take breaks every two hours for self-care activities like a walk, meditation, or even just a few deep breaths. Push the reset button!
Checking emails every hour	Create a schedule of checking emails twice per day, and let people know with an auto-responder what times I am checking!
Not sure what my priorities are	Realign my priorities every day to match what is going on
Multitasking	Just DON'T
No time to think straight, just so BUSY!	Create white space for the unexpected, big-picture thinking, innovation, and processing

CHAPTER 7

THE BUSY BAROMETER

What Gets Measured Gets Improved

Billy Beane was the general manager of the Oakland Athletics baseball team in the early 2000s. After losing several players to free agency, he was faced with the need to rebuild on a limited budget. He rejected the traditional way of evaluating players and instead used an unusual and very modern method called "sabermetrics," which used a far wider variety of data to make the assessments. If you are an avid reader of business literature or a fan of Jonah Hill or Brad Pitt, you may remember the book or movie *Moneyball* telling this story.

The basic theme of the tale was already stated years before by management theorist Peter Drucker: "What gets measured gets improved."

Measurement permeates every aspect of human life. We wear Fitbits or Apple watches to measure our heart rate, oxygen consumption, calorie burn, and steps. Yet none of these devices measure our Busyness, or our happiness. And it's critical to measure those as well.

It is only when our measurement tools malfunction or are unavailable that we begin to appreciate how important they are. Just last week my niece's diabetes monitor was not working properly, and her sugar started to crash. Luckily, she is a nurse who works in an emergency room, where they are trained to recognize insulin issues. She was able to get the care she needed.

Here's the reality: if we were to try to live without measurement for even a single day, we would quickly see just how vital measurement is and what gets measured in our everyday lives.

Without measurement, there would be no clocks or alarms to awaken you at a selected time. After you woke up, you could not use the stovetop, oven, or microwave to make breakfast or coffee. All these devices rely on measurements of temperature or time to heat food and beverages. Nor could you use a modern refrigerator since it requires measurement to keep food and beverages at a preset temperature.

You could not drive to work because modern automobiles use onboard computers, which rely on measurement to control the ignition system, automatic transmission, brakes, engine temperature, throttle position, and mix of fuel and oxygen. Even if you could drive a car, you could never know how fast you were going because you would not have a speedometer.

At work, you could not use a computer, since computers require measurement to operate. Nor could you use a landline telephone, cell phone, or fax machine to communicate with others because these devices rely on measurement to operate.

Forget about flying, or taking a bus, train, or ocean liner on an intercontinental business trip, and forget about traveling overseas. Long-distance transportation and navigation would be impossible without the measurement of distance, speed, time, direction, and fuel.

Businesses today use all kinds of methods to measure their success, including OKRs, KPIs, and business scorecards.

But how can we measure Busyness? It usually comes down to the subjective feeling of being busy. Busy or not busy is too black and white. It doesn't get at the shades of gray or the different reasons you are stuck in the daily grind and not able to focus on what's truly important.

Without a score, how will you know if you're improving? More importantly, what are the things that contribute to your Busyness, the specific catalysts?

For that purpose, with the help of a tremendous amount of research, many human resource managers, and an industrial engineer, I have created the Busy Barometer, a five-minute survey that helps identify what low-value things can be eliminated from your life.

You can take the Busy Barometer survey in the next section of this chapter and then enter your answers online to get your score: **peggysullivanspeaker.com/busy-barometer**

I took a team at Google through this program, and here is what German Santana, their team leader and manager of revenue at the company, told me:

> *We are more than grateful for your unique approach to escaping the Busyness trap. Your process is extremely effective in helping individuals achieve more with less. I have begun incorporating the Busy Barometer in my*

*own life and am already finding more time for what's
important. I highly recommend the barometer to anyone who is looking to improve their time management
skills and quality of life.*

Regardless, you should read the rest of this chapter to understand the more than twenty different types of busy traps I have
identified, with the help of psychologists, HR managers, and industrial psychologists—and how to bust them.

YOUR SUITCASE WON'T ZIP IF YOU'VE OVERPACKED

The zipper broke as I was trying to close the suitcase. I took everything out and ran into my basement to get a bigger one. But my
husband had moved the bags, and I couldn't find what I was looking
for. As a result, I missed my flight. The event was three days long,
so I did manage to attend most of it. But why had I waited till the
last minute to pack?

When we're busy, we can easily end up doing things in a rush.
We don't factor in time for accidents or errors and end up losing
ten times as many hours.

The Busy Barometer asks you questions that explore your habits
so you can avoid the most common busy traps. The first part of the
survey (questions 1–8) deals with overpacking our schedules, priority setting, multitasking, and how we tackle larger projects. The
next group of questions (9–15) focuses on self-care, physical and
mental health, and pushing the reset button. The last section (questions 16–22) focuses on communication, connection, meeting management, ability to delegate, and aligning our core capabilities with
our work.

The Busy Barometer assessment that follows will identify some of the potholes that are getting in the way of your productivity. If you answer "majority of the time" or "sometimes" to any of the questions, it is likely you are in the throes of a low-value activity.

Remember that you must visit my website at
peggysullivanspeaker.com/busy-barometer
and enter your answers there to calculate your score!

Busy Barometer Survey

Please rate the following based on your experience over the past few months.

○○○				
	Majority of the time	Sometimes	Rarely	Never
1. Do you end each day feeling you did NOT have time for what's important?				

HABITS/FOCUS/PRIORITIES/PRODUCTIVITY/
MULTITASKING/PROCRASTINATION

Please rate the following based on your experience over the past few months.

	Majority of the time	Sometimes	Rarely	Never
2. Is your schedule filled most days?				
3. Do you feel so rushed that you have little time to prepare for important events or meetings?				
4. Do you routinely end the day with extra work that takes time away from what you enjoy?				
5. Do you struggle to set your daily priorities?				
6. Is multitasking a core strategy for getting your work done?				
7. Do you mostly focus on easy things to cross them off the list?				
8. When focusing on big projects, do you feel overwhelmed or unable to break them down into smaller pieces?				

HEALTH/SELF-CARE/SLEEP/NUTRITION/MENTAL HEALTH/PUSHING RESET

Please rate the following based on your experience over the past few months.

	Majority of the time	Sometimes	Rarely	Never
9. Is your sleep suffering because your mind is too focused on your to-do list or you are too busy to get enough sleep?				
10. Do good nutrition and physical movement suffer during the day?				
11. Do you feel overwhelmed, stressed, or struggle with your mental health?				
12. Do you get to the end of the day without regular breaks to eat and recharge?				
13. Is it difficult to keep up with routine tasks like haircuts, doctors' appointments, or shopping?				
14. Do you skip vacations and holidays?				
15. Does your sense of purpose or values get lost?				

COMMUNICATION/CONNECTION/MEETINGS/ DELEGATION/STRENGTHS

Please rate the following based on your experience over the past few months.

	Majority of the time	Sometimes	Rarely	Never
16. Is it difficult to find time for meaningful relationships (family, friends, community)?				
17. Do you attend meetings where there is no clear goal, objective, or next steps?				
18. Are you interrupted with calls and messages?				
19. Is it difficult to return calls, emails, or messages in a timely manner?				
20. Do you look at your email and other messages so often that you can't get work done?				
21. Do your activities fail to align with your strengths and likes?				
22. Do you find it easier to do something yourself rather than ask for help?				

BUSY BAROMETER SCORE CATEGORIES

Score	Definition
86–100	Congratulations! You are a master of your time! Being a master of your time means taking control of your life instead of constantly being controlled by external forces. Stay consistent with your habits. Look at these additional ways you can become even more effective.
75–85	Congratulations! You are mastering your time well but could improve. Work on these specific suggestions to become even more effective.
51–74	You need to focus more on your priorities, manage distractions, and take care of your mental and physical health. Work on these suggestions to improve your score.
0–50	You are not making conscious choices to focus on your priorities, manage distractions and take care of your mental and physical health. Work on these suggestions to improve your score.

MICROSTEPS MAKE IT EASY
—EVOLUTION, NOT REVOLUTION

Elle spent her twenties living up to her family's expectations and her thirties raising her children while building her career. By the time she reached her forties, she didn't know who she was. She was busy doing things she didn't care about at all. She felt unfulfilled and depressed most of the time.

She went to see a battery of doctors and counselors until she finally reached a simple understanding: her life sucked. And it had sucked for more than two decades. It had been way too long since she looked at her authentic self to focus on what she wanted and needed.

How could she dig herself out of such a pit? It seemed too deep and dark to escape from. Elle's family thought she was just lazy. Elle even began to believe them. But she wasn't lazy. She was busy. The list of what she wanted to do to catch up with her lost past was pages long. Most of all she wanted to travel. But the list was so long she couldn't make sense of it, and as a result, she could barely leave her house.

Elle's therapist advised her to take microsteps. "Start with the easiest thing," she said. "Just write about your desires in your journal." Two weeks later, she suggested Elle do the same thing but in a café. By the end of the month, she suggested Elle take a day trip to one of the nearby places she'd always wanted to go. Within a few months, Elle traveled out of the country.

When January came, Elle was not just surviving—she was also delighted. She brightened every room she stepped into. She had busted her Busyness. But not overnight. Not all at once.

The truth is, Elle found it difficult to step out of her comfort zone. Her Busyness drained her, but it was also much like a safety blanket. Getting herself to take drastic action to change things was never going to work. Microsteps were the solution.

The advice in books like this is usually to think big. But progress is often easier when you think small and steady than to try to do everything all at once.

Microsteps help overcome entropy and resistance. It's easier to move an inch than a mile. Just make sure you're moving, and all will be well.

You will notice that every question has a number. Go back and look at your answers on Pages 100-104.

For each "majority of the time," "sometimes," or "rarely" answer that you gave in the Busy Barometer survey, the bullets beneath the questions in the section that follows provide you with one microstep you can take to improve the situation. If you gave those answers to more than two questions in each section, pick no more than two at a time to focus on.

1. **Do you end each day feeling you do not have time for what is important?**
    Very few escape the feeling of time poverty—not having time for what is important. Busy traps snarl the best of us. Questions 2-22 will help you identify your individual habits and patterns so you can break free and focus on what is truly important.

HABITS/FOCUS/PRIORITIES/MULTITASKING AND PROCRASTINATION

2. **Is your schedule filled most days?**
    Leave at least 25 percent of your day open for getting your work done or deal with unanticipated events.

3. **Do you feel so rushed that you have little time to prepare for important events or meetings?**
    Spend at least thirty minutes regularly preparing for your scheduled events.

4. **Do you routinely end the day with extra work that takes time away from what you enjoy?**
    Leave at least 25 percent of your day to focus on your priorities.

5. **Do you struggle to set your daily priorities?**
    Spend fifteen minutes picking your top 1–3 priorities.

6. **Is multitasking a core strategy for getting your work done?**
    Stop multitasking any high-value activities. It takes longer.

7. **Do you mostly focus on easy things to cross them off the list?**
    Focus on your priorities first, not the easy stuff, or you won't have time left for the important things.

8. **When focusing on big projects, do you feel overwhelmed or unable to break them down into smaller pieces?**
    Break your big projects into doable steps.

HEALTH/SELF-CARE/SLEEP/NUTRITION/MENTAL HEALTH AND PUSHING RESET

9. **Is your sleep suffering because your mind is too focused on your to-do list or are too busy to get enough sleep?**
    Get at least seven hours of sleep per night. Try breathing exercises or meditation to ease into sleep.

10. **Do good nutrition and physical movement suffer during the day?**
    Preplan your meals and physically move through your day.

11. **Do you feel overwhelmed, stressed, or struggle with your mental health?**

    Explore the reason you may feel stressed. Remember, there are some things you cannot control. Talk to a qualified professional.

12. **Do you get to the end of the day without regular breaks to eat and recharge?**

    Set regular breaks throughout the day (going for a walk or eating a treat).

13. **Is it difficult to keep up with routine tasks like haircuts, doctors' appointments, or shopping?**

    Schedule time for routine tasks. Only cancel in emergencies.

14. **Do you skip vacations and holidays?**

    Take your vacations and holidays. When you take from your gas tank, you need to replenish.

15. **Does your sense of purpose or values get lost?**

    Determine your core values. Evaluate on a regular basis whether or not you are living them. When one is missing, focus on it the next day.

COMMUNICATION/CONNECTION/MEETINGS/ DELEGATION/STRENGTHS

16. **Is it difficult to find time for meaningful relationships (family, friends, community)?**

    Set aside time for the relationships you value. Eliminate the time you spend with things/people who you don't value or learn from.

17. **Do you attend meetings where there is no clear goal, objective, or next steps?**

    Make sure every meeting or gathering you go to has a clear purpose and your presence is necessary. Ensure every gathering has the next steps articulated.

18. **Are you interrupted by calls and messages?**

    Block out media free time and communicate to your community what they are.

19. **Is it difficult to return calls, emails, or messages in a timely manner?**

    Set aside time to return important calls and messages routinely in your day.

20. **Do you look at your email and other messages so often that you can't get work done?**

    Set up routine times to review messages. Communicate your schedule with key community members.

21. **Do your activities fail to align with your strengths and likes?**

Before starting an activity, evaluate if it's a good use of time based on your priorities/strengths. If not, seek an alternative method to complete it.

22. **Do you find it easier to do something yourself rather than ask for help?**

Get accustomed to asking for help so you can free up your time for what's important.

BUSY-BUSTING TOOL #7

Develop a List of Your Favorite Happy Memories

We all get lost in low-value activities. Here is another way to get you back on track.

For each of these memories, try to recall how it made you feel emotionally, physically, and spiritually.

Memory	Emotional	Physical	Spiritual

Develop a list of your best memories—moments of pride, happiness, and satisfaction. Write it down and think of how it made you feel emotionally, physically, and spiritually. When you feel that life has knocked the wind out of you, think about this memory and work to bring those good feelings back to life.

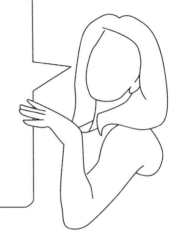

Moments of Pride, Happiness, and Satisfaction:

- Running my first marathon at age fifty: I can do anything I set my mind to. Age is just a number.

- Caring for and nursing my terminally ill mother: Grateful I could help in her darkest hour.

- Having my son: What a miracle. The best thing I ever did.

- Marrying my second husband: Lucky me. He is a good man. He makes me laugh.

The list might have ten entries or a hundred. You can keep adding to the list as you think of more examples.

Why create this list? You can bring back memories and experience them again. If you focus on the way they made you feel, you can bring up that feeling again!

When you feel yourself getting busy, think about a memory from this list, and remind yourself there is more to life than just getting things done.

CHAPTER 8

MOJO MAKING—MAKE YOURSELF HAPPY ON PURPOSE

Chelsea's doctor told her she needed to make radical changes or else. She was 110 pounds overweight, her blood pressure was off the charts, and she was in danger of multiple medical complications. She needed to eat better and exercise, of course. But when could she find the time to cook or go to the gym? She worked sixty to eighty hours every week, and when she finished her workday, she was exhausted.

The doctor said it was up to her. She could change her life or keep spiraling toward an early death.

Her physical health wasn't her only problem. To put it bluntly, Chelsea was unhappy. She couldn't remember the last time she actually felt good about her life or herself. When a good friend pointed out there might be a link between her mood and her physical condition, Chelsea was stunned. Of course, there was a link. It was obvious.

Her overall lack of physical and mental well-being was making her ill. Being sick was making her miserable. Or was being miserable making her ill? That same day she realized this, she went out for a walk in the park. She couldn't even make it half a mile. But she did feel a little bit better. It was a start.

This small first step soon grew, and Chelsea's life began to transform. Within a month she was walking two miles every night. She also added a short morning yoga practice.

Four years later, Chelsea is no longer overweight by even one pound. She walks five miles every day. She advocates for other people to focus on their wellness. She is no longer addicted to Busyness. Now she is addicted, as she puts it, "to movement and endorphins." But most of all, she is addicted to happiness.

There are three steps in the Busy-Busting Process. This chapter is all about step two: the massive momentous magic of Mojo Making.

MOJO MAKING REQUIRES INTENTION

Joy does not come falling out of the sky. Sure, sometimes amazing things happen without effort. But most of the time, you have to build magic one block at a time.

My friend Kate Glaser is a media personality whose life revolves around Mojo Making: "Making people happy is part of my life's work. My company, Hope Rises, its entire brand is built around this."

As a former journalist, Kate knows it's important to be up to date on the news—even the bad stuff. But it's also important to have somewhere to go for uplifting, positive stories. That's what her nonprofit, Hope Rises, does—it shares stories that celebrate compassion, love, strength, inspiration, and hope.

"We do not just tell good news," Kate said. "We make good news happen."

It's impossible not to be inspired when you hear a story about a good deed. A sick girl's bike was stolen, and upon hearing this, a stranger quietly gifts her a new one. A boy who loves country music and is in the middle of very rough cancer treatment gets taken to a Luke Bryan concert. A terminal sheltered dog gets to spend his last days with a loving family instead of the overcrowded facility in which he has spent too much of his life.

These stories ignite us; they make us feel good. The comment sections of the Hope Rises social media pages stand as a testament to the far-reaching effect of doing good and giving back.

"People love happy stories. It brings out the best in them," Kate said.

Happiness is not an object. It is not a destination. It is not a result. Happiness is a journey, a series of micromoments we pass through. That's the essence of Mojo Making: creating intentional acts of happiness that are repeatable. The benefit of doing so is incredibly gratifying in terms of improved energy, productivity, and overall quality of life.

There are four important steps in Mojo Making:

1. Determining Your Nonnegotiables
2. Focusing on Self-Care
3. Creating Happiness Rituals
4. Becoming a Mojo Maker for Others

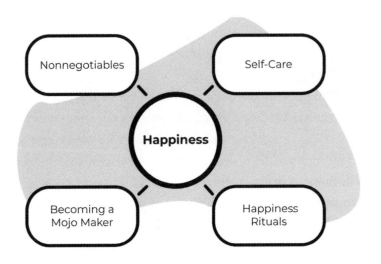

MOJO MAKING STEP ONE
—DECLARE YOUR NONNEGOTIABLES

When he was thirteen, my dad got his first job standing outside a grocery store pulling wagons of groceries for the neighborhood because no one had cars. He earned a quarter per wagon and on a good week would make twenty dollars, which helped with family expenses.

The pressure to help pay for his family necessities drove him to eat, work, sleep, and repeat at a very young age. He developed this addiction early and carried it for nearly sixty years. While the mantra of eat, work, sleep is not hereditary, in retrospect I learned a lot about this type of behavior from my dad. While he made a life for himself and his family, there was far too little quality of life.

When my mom died, though, my father realized he had not been the father and husband he had wanted to be because his work kept him too busy. So at sixty-two years old, he cut back on his work and started doing the things he loved. He called them his "nonnegotiables."

He started to play bridge. He went on cruises three or four times a year. He never missed his weekly dinners with me after that point. Every day he made it a point to regularly do the things that gave him joy. He died at eighty-eight, twenty-six years after making this choice. He accomplished a *lot* of happiness in that time. On his deathbed he told me his only regret in life was not declaring and taking his nonnegotiables earlier. But he still had nearly three decades of living them fully.

Your nonnegotiables are the things you need and want in life. They change throughout the various cycles of life. But at any given time, they are absolute—the things you must have in place to live your best life. Clearly knowing what these things are and measuring them is critical to your quality of life. They are the things you need to do to feel your best.

Your nonnegotiables are sacred. They are not open to discussion or negotiation. They ignite your power and make you unstoppable. When you hold to your nonnegotiables, you become more effective, successful, and most important—happier.

Nonnegotiables are not about having control. Rather, they are about the power of choice. They are essential to start down the road of happiness. You can't be a Mojo Maker without standing for your nonnegotiables. When you let your nonnegotiables slip, Busyness creeps back in.

Just consider the case of Lauren Simonetti:

> *One day I locked my four-year-old son in the car. I had a toddler and newborn and a busy job at Fox. We had*

also just moved into a home and were trying to settle in. I had someone coming to hang curtains. That day I got up early and shoveled the driveway as it was snowing hard. I got in the car and drove my son to a birthday party. I had not planned on staying at the party, just dropping my son off.

I was parked badly, so I wanted to be quick. I grabbed the gift for the birthday boy and knocked on the door. The mother of the birthday boy was surprised I was not going to stay, but I was busy and had my day productively organized. I went back to the car to get my son and realized I was locked out of the car, and my son was still in it.

To make it even worse, it was still snowing. I looked for the keys and could not find them. I was in sheer panic. I looked and looked and looked and could not find them. Too late I realized I should have canceled the curtains. My son is my priority, but I was trying to be a superwoman. I should have asked for help. Ultimately, I found the keys in the gift bag. But it was a horrible, horrible experience. My Busyness and need to get stuff done made me lose sight of my priorities.

Nonnegotiables come in every shape and size. They are not the same for your relationships with friends as they are for your relationships with family. They are not the same in romance as they are at work.

The easiest way to manage nonnegotiables is to schedule them into your day as you would do with any important appointment.

They can be as simple as taking a break every hour for five minutes or taking time before bed to make a gratitude list.

My daily nonnegotiables keep me focused, successful, and healthy, no matter what the external circumstances. Staying true to my daily nonnegotiables is my first nonnegotiable.

PEGGY'S BUSY-BUSTING NONNEGOTIABLES

1. Sleep at least eight hours every night.
2. Never skip breakfast and especially not coffee.
3. Movement daily. At least three days with weights and three days of hot power yoga.
4. Eat healthfully 90 percent of the time and enjoy my 10 percent off.
5. Take my cat, Oliver, for a walk in his buggy. Make him walk at least one full block on his own. Or letting him crawl on my belly, wrap his paws around me, and purr against my heartbeat.
6. Tell my husband or at least think about telling him how much I love him and how happy I am with him in my life.
7. Count my blessings daily.
8. Do a random act of kindness regularly.
9. Think of my mother, father, and son, sometimes ex-husband.
10. Be silly.

There are three types of nonnegotiables, each equally important.

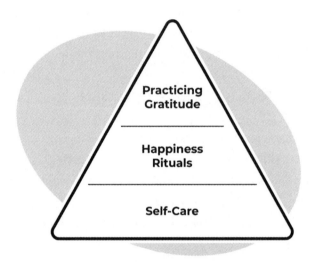

1. PRACTICING GRATITUDE

Count your blessings and give back generously.

2. HAPPINESS RITUALS

Things you do because they give you joy. We will explain more later in the chapter.

3. SELF-CARE

Doing what provides optimal physical, mental, spiritual, and emotional well-being.

I deal with each of these in the pages that follow.

SELF-CARE MATTERS MOST

Ashley never knew that she was living in the fast lane until the COVID-19 pandemic hit. She was running a business during the day, teaching online in the early mornings, serving on an executive board for a nonprofit organization, writing a book, and mothering her second grader, all while her new husband and she were trying to conceive a second baby. It all seemed just fine to her.

But when the country went into lockdown, everything got turned upside down. As everyone tried to adapt to the health crisis, many areas of Ashley's life screamed for 100 percent of her attention and time all at once. Something had to give. She ditched writing her book to create accelerated marketing campaigns for clients. She stopped teaching online to attend more meetings. She put her own marketing aside to train my nonprofit SheCAN! on how to pivot to an online model.

Soon, she realized she was filling everyone else's buckets, leaving hers completely empty. She developed a short fuse and high anxiety, and she started experiencing fertility issues.

Finally, sitting in her home office, she broke down. She sat sobbing, staring at her project management system, SheCAN!'s meeting schedule, her son's homeschool curriculum, the outline for her book, and her orders for fertility treatments. It was too much to manage.

She suddenly realized she could not be a good mother, wife, employee, or business owner if she was falling to pieces. She had to let go of anything that wasn't serving her.

She opened a notebook and wrote down her core values: family, creativity, and freedom. She then listed everything in her life. Those things that aligned with her core values, she circled. Those that didn't, she crossed off the list.

Suddenly, she saw the way forward: a life created, each day, as an act of intention. At first she thought it would be difficult to execute. But it was easy, actually. She canceled early morning meetings and replaced them with writing and yoga. She stopped trading her hours for dollars and delegated things that didn't align with her values.

It was just a matter of giving herself permission to put herself first.

Your attitude determines your altitude. A positive attitude leads to success. And the best way to be positive is to take care of yourself. If you wait for the free champagne tomorrow, you will never make it to the toast.

Like many women, I am a natural caregiver. So I forgive myself for having spent years rationalizing not focusing on self-care. I used to think self-care is selfish. But it is not. There is a reason that self-care is a ten-billion-dollar industry.

Now by self-care, I do not mean taking a spa day or spending Saturday on a Netflix binge while drinking pumpkin spice latte. That's nice, but the self-care I am talking about is the daily, intentional process of sustaining your mental, physical, emotional, and physical health.

While the concept of self-care seems simple, it is important to note the five types:

Quiet Space	Child's Play
Lifestyle	Growth
Me Time	

Types of Self-Care

QUIET SPACE

In a world where nothing stops moving, it is critical to take some time to reflect, debrief, and sit with yourself. I take five minutes every day to recalibrate at the end of the day and make sure I am laser focused on what my priorities are for the next day.

Time spent in reflection is important; it allows us to recalibrate and recharge. It gives us space and conscious attention to deal with the unexpected. It allows us to figure out what we are feeling. I take time every night to check through my most important values and ensure I am living on purpose. If I discover I am not, I make adjustments on the spot.

CHILD'S PLAY

Yes, playtime. My favorite play buddy is my cat, Oliver. We engage in a lot of play during his daily walk. I recently started bringing my nine-year-old and six-year-old neighbors along. What a sense of wonderment they have. It's intoxicating and highly contagious; they have me skipping, running, and hopping with them. Game changing.

LIFESTYLE
Nutrition, exercise, rest. Simple.

GROWTH
My father used to say a day without learning something new is a lost opportunity. Challenging yourself, setting the bar high, enables growth. If I do not feel a bit of discomfort every day, I know I am doing something wrong.

ME TIME
I have always enjoyed a successful career and lived an amazing professional life, with a big salary, authority, and travels around the world. It looked great from the outside, but in reality, I had few friends and no safe place to turn for comfort.

What if we took just five minutes of rest every hour? It's enough. That's almost two hours a day of relaxation, without even noticing it. Even with self-care, microsteps work. Me time is your time. Don't miss it.

HAPPINESS RITUALS—MAKE JOY AN ACTION
I was in Los Angeles not too long ago for a big meeting. I was prepared but still anxious. I was tired. I had not slept the night before. The TV in the room next to me was blaring, and my room was way too cold. I knew I needed to do something to improve my energy level. So I grabbed my laptop, found a neighborhood coffee shop, and indulged in one of my favorite happiness rituals. I closed my eyes, took a deep breath, and went for it.

Mmmmm. When I opened my eyes, everyone in the coffee shop was staring at me. Come on! Hadn't they ever seen someone having taste-bud orgasms while slowly relishing a couple of pieces of Dove Dark Chocolate before? I was moaning pretty loud, I guess. But I was fully enjoying the pleasure is the point of my Dove Dark Chocolate happiness ritual.

Every morning before I start working, I light pumpkin spice candles. They remind me of Halloween with my father.

When working, I often put on my fuzzy pink slippers—they keep my feet warm, but the real joy is, they look ridiculous, so they make me smile.

Happiness rituals are consistent habits and behaviors that evoke joy, generate energy, drive endorphins, and make you feel connected. They're like a reset button that brings you to a joyous state that makes even the biggest metaphorical mountain look like a walk in the park. I like to do them several times a day.

Happiness is like a muscle—the more you flex it, the stronger it gets. The better you feel, the easier it is for you to take action aligned with your values and your purpose instead of being driven by the goals or demands that drive you back into Busyness.

Happiness rituals are as unique as fingerprints. Everyone has their own set of practices to light them up. Drink chamomile tea. Scratch your dog's belly. Go out for a beer with your brother. Give a homeless person near your house a donut. Whatever it is, get it going.

○○○

Here are a few suggestions for Happiness Rituals people I know have used effectively:

- ☐ Take a short walk every few hours. Changing your scenery can change everything.

- ☐ Shift your point of view. A fresh perspective is as good as a brand new day.

- ☐ Three times a day, Google a clip from your favorite TV series and watch it.

- ☐ Count your blessings. Literally. A gratitude list.

- ☐ Meditate. Deep breathing readjusts your nervous system.

- ☐ Color. I bought a cat's butt coloring book. Ten minutes of coloring and everything looks better - especially when you are coloring a cat's butt.

- ☐ Make a call every day to a friend you haven't spoken to in a while. Ask how they are - and hope their answer isn't "Busy!"

BECOME A MOJO MAKER FOR OTHERS
—FOR GIVING IS BETTER THAN RECEIVING

When my son was two years old, he loved making scrambled eggs for dinner. He would crack the eggs into the pan and stand on the stool to cook them. One evening he wanted to make eggs, but we were out. I was annoyed because he was making a ruckus while I was trying to have a phone call with my mother. My mother had advanced cancer at this point, and every conversation with her mattered.

Imagine my surprise when the doorbell rang twenty minutes later, and I found my mother standing on the porch holding a carton of eggs. Even sick, she went to the shop to get eggs and brought them over so my son could fulfill his evening ritual.

She died just a few weeks later, and I will never forget that moment. At her funeral, every person told stories of how she was the kindest person they had ever known. How she made them feel welcome. On the day of her funeral, I took a vow to always honor her by trying to be as kind as she was.

In a world where you can be anything, be generous. People will remember your generosity.

The easiest way to make mojo for others is to surround yourself with people who are Mojo Makers as well. The synergy will spiral your mutual happiness up and up and up. When we are amid people who motivate us, their energy is contagious and gives us a sense that anything is possible. Birds of a feather flock together.

BUSY-BUSTING TOOL #8

Get Your Mojo Making in Motion

Make a list of things you do or can start doing to get your endorphins going.

List three to five actions under each of the following steps:

Declare Your Nonnegotiables

1.
2.
3.
4.
5.

Practice Happiness Rituals

1.
2.
3.
4.
5.

Acts of Self-Care

1.
2.
3.
4.
5.

Become a Mojo Maker for Others

1.
2.
3.
4.
5.

Next, pick one action from each list that you will do immediately, and put those four into your calendar for the next four days, one per day.

Then do the same with all the listed items—pick one to put into your calendar to achieve each day.

If any of these actions require follow-up, in other words, if they demand multiple days to be addressed, put the follow-ups into your calendar as well.

Once you have taken each action, write about the results in your journal. The results include both what you cause out there in the real world and what you cause in the emotions of the people around you—and also very importantly, the results you cause in your own thoughts and feelings. How do these actions impact your sense of being too busy?

CHAPTER 9

VALUES VIBING

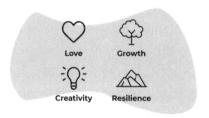

I wasn't wearing underwear at the opening session of our first SheCAN! Summit. But I'll get to that in a moment.

The summit was amazing. Badass women flew in from all over America to grow, thrive, vibe, and find solutions to the challenges women face today. Coming out of COVID-19, this was the first opportunity in more than two years for these women to come together.

I had just returned from a three-day speaking engagement. As psyched as I was for the cocktail party opening for the summit, I was also exhausted. In the car driving over, I kept thinking I was missing something, but I scanned my checklist several times, and everything was fine. When I rushed into the room, I passed a floor air unit and felt a draft go up my legs, and suddenly, it hit me: what was missing was my panties. Busyness had struck again!

This time though, I brought everything I learned over the years to bear and pulled myself into the present. The event was starting, and I could do nothing about my commando situation right now. It was time to start the icebreaker I had prepared, where each woman would tell us a little about herself followed by a fun fact.

As the host, I got to go last. This was great, and I was grateful because with the underwear situation, I could not recall the fun fact I had memorized. One woman announced, "Fun fact: I'm pregnant!" Another had just put out a documentary about human trafficking.

When it was my turn, I blurted out, "I am not wearing underwear!" Everybody burst into wild laughter. Now that was both badass—and bareass! It set my credentials up perfectly for the next day, when I led a values workshop. I've run this workshop dozens of times with a diverse range of groups. But this time was really special because I was leading it for my own organization. I was getting to share my Beyond Busy model with my people as a group for the first time.

Actually, I had spent years workshopping and surveying women about what values or combination of them would result in maximum quality of life. At the time I had presented hundreds of workshops on the topic. I knew the answers to the question because thousands of women had told me. The key to living your life comes down to the four value clusters I shared earlier: connection, energy, growth mindset, and authenticity.

In this chapter we will look at how to most effectively unpack these four value clusters to live your best life.

CONNECTION IS NOT ABOUT THE INTERNET—FAMILY, COMMUNITY, LOVE, RELATIONSHIPS, TEAMWORK

Once when I was shopping for groceries, I saw a woman in her nineties struggle with her cart. I asked if I could help her. She was taken aback. She said, "I don't walk really well, and I can't reach the upper shelves. Yes, help would be appreciated."

Her name was Sally. In the hour I spent with her that day, I learned why bananas bruise, how to find the perfect dent-free can of tuna, and how much fat ground beef needs to make the perfect meatloaf. When it was time to pay, Sally fumbled in her purse for food stamps and a few small coins. She told the clerk at the register, "Ring these important things first. I can't afford all of it." I stepped in front of Sally, gave the clerk my credit card, and told Sally it was on me.

Sally cried then. She was so grateful for my assistance, and now this on top of it. Sally told me how difficult it was for her to shop on her own, and her family didn't live close enough to help regularly. So I gave her a business card and told her to call me anytime she needed to shop.

When I got home, my husband said, "Where are the groceries?" I had gotten so inspired by helping Sally I totally forgot my own shopping.

The next day Sally's relatives from out of town started to call me. Her grandchildren, her children, her sisters, on and on. "Sally can't stop talking about the kind deed." "You made Sally's month." My "helper's high" lasted for weeks, and I couldn't wait to take her shopping again. So much better than the dopamine shot of my Busyness addiction.

Connection is critical to life. Connection gives life meaning. Of course, I am not talking about surfing the internet. I'm talking about people, not technology. Connection means love and family but also much more than that. Connection reinforces our diversity, reminding us we are exactly like everyone else and yet totally different.

Connection also means community. I go to Florida every year for a few months. Whenever I get back to Buffalo and go to yoga class, as soon as I walk in the door, I get smiles and hugs from all the people who have missed my presence. It feels so amazing to feel part of that. They are my people, my community.

Another important element of connection is connection to myself. That's where self-love comes into play. It could be as simple as sitting down and looking back at my life and feeling proud about something or even just looking at the past day and saying to myself, "What did I do well?" and giving myself credit for that. Giving myself kudos has come a lot easier since I realized that it is about progress, not perfection.

ENERGY MANAGEMENT IS A SKILL—PHYSICAL, MENTAL, EMOTIONAL, AND SPIRITUAL WELLNESS

Jennifer woke up exhausted every single day. Her Apple Watch insisted she had lain there for seven hours every night, but she felt like she hadn't slept in years. Her boss demanded earlier and earlier mornings and later and later nights.

By now Jennifer regularly started her workday from home before her two children even woke up. When they got on the school bus, she would drive to the office for what felt like a second shift at the same time everyone else started their whole day. No time for breakfast at all, and when lunch came, she ate a sandwich with one hand while continuing to type with the other, sometimes managing client calls by tucking her phone under her chin. Her lunch was usually a peanut butter and jelly sandwich, even though she was gluten intolerant, because it was easier to make a third sandwich than try to create something healthier just for herself.

After work she would pick up her kids at day care, take them to soccer practice and dance lessons, and shop for groceries. By the time they got home, it was usually after 7:00 p.m., and her kids were overstimulated and didn't want to sleep at all. They ran laps around the dining room table while she cooked them macaroni and cheese or made more sandwiches.

Eventually, of course, Jennifer had a meltdown, triggered by something simple: she tripped over a pile of unwashed laundry. No big deal. But it was because she couldn't get up. She just lay there watching her kids eat their KFC, listening to the emails from work pinging through her inbox.

Enough was enough.

When she finally managed to stand up, Jennifer called her best friend. Together, they agreed she needed to find a way to regain her energy. The first step she committed to was to make her own lunches, focused on macronutrients and keeping it above-all reasonably healthy. Next, she started actually eating it during an actual lunch *break*. She stopped working from home in the mornings. She was scared losing these three or four hours a day would bury her, but she had no choice.

Jennifer was stunned to realize that her productivity quickly increased. She was working much faster, making fewer errors. By cutting her work time and focusing on maximizing her energy, she had freed herself from the Busyness cycle. Since then, Jennifer has added an evening yoga session after her children go to sleep. She has lost ten pounds and feels fantastic. I find Jennifer's story empowering and inspiring beyond measure. Energy is everything.

But energy management is not just about sleep and diet and exercise. It's also about attitude.

Negative thinking wastes vast amounts of energy. So whenever a negative thought arises, I let go of it fast. I replace it with fun and humor. I sing out loud on my daily walks. I don't care if I'm out of tune. Playful makes me present, and being present jacks up my energy even more.

Managing your energy also means downtime. We don't expect a toy to run without batteries, yet we'll sit for hours trying to get a job done without even getting up once. When I was still in full-blown active Busyness addiction, I would forget to take a break until I would get so stuck and remember that a bit of distraction might just solve everything. It almost always does.

Managing energy requires discipline. And discipline is easy when we're living our values. When I remember that energy is of core importance, it is much simpler to remember to manage it. Try doing less and watch your energy soar. Managing your energy is a core value for living your best life.

DON'T GO A DAY WITHOUT GROWTH
—OPEN-MINDEDNESS, NONJUDGMENT, CURIOSITY

When I went back into the working world after my mother passed away, at Blue Cross, the person who hired me was in a different city. The very first day that I was there, it was a Friday, and people left early, and I had nobody to onboard me. This was thirty years ago, when we were just getting started with computers.

So from her remote location, my supervisor gave me one simple task: put out a group communication to the entire organization. I didn't even know where the group email address book was. I barely even understood email at that point. There was nobody there to even tell me which computer to use or how to turn it on.

So I sat there trying to figure this all out, until that night. In walked this really tall gentleman. He asked me who I was. I introduced myself and told him it was my first day and what I was trying—and failing—to accomplish. He told me he was new to the company too, and he, too, had a problem.

"You see this welcome packet?" he asked me and held out an envelope with like a thousand brochures poking out, all different sizes and shapes. He dumped them in a pile on the desk in front of us. "I want to initiate my health plan. I want to know how to activate my benefits. But I mean, how do I even begin? This is a health-care organization. Every customer should know how to access and understand their benefits. This pile of stuff makes it too hard."

This looked like a challenge I could have a go at. "Let me try to sort this out," I told him.

When I came in on Monday, I discovered that guy was the new CEO. Holy crap, I thought. This was an opportunity to add real value. So I created an innovation called the Blue Pages, a directory that outlined member benefits in an easy-to-use format similar to the yellow pages. At the time it was so novel that it won a national competition. Suddenly, I was a superstar in an area that wasn't even in my job description.

Next thing I knew, I was marketing director and, soon after that, VP of marketing. That threw me into a whole new cycle of Busyness. But that's another story.

The point is, I succeeded in this job because I was curious. And boy did I have to travel way outside my comfort zone. I was new to the health-care industry and had to learn it pronto. I wanted to know how to solve the problem that was presented to me even though it wasn't supposed to be my task. It was a struggle because there was so much health-care language and details of the regulations, and it involved a lot of departments. It was honestly a bear of a project. But I stuck with it because I wanted to solve it.

Curiosity requires a strong growth mindset. A growth mindset opens opportunities. It makes the mundane exciting. It helps you meet new people. It teaches you to find victory in every challenge and a lesson in every failure.

A growth mindset leads to opportunity. It fosters both personal and professional growth. It builds empathy and helps you be interested in people around you. It kills monotony—you will never be bored again.

It also encourages an attitude of nonjudgment and open-mindedness that makes us attractive to other people.

Dare I say one more time my dad's favorite saying: "A day without learning something new is a lost opportunity." Thanks, Dad, for teaching me this at such a young age.

AUTHENTICITY IS EVERYTHING!
RESIST THE PRESSURE TO CONFORM

When Julie Zhu came home on a cold night in 2019, she read an email from the company that was going to hire her. They changed their minds at the last minute. Suddenly, she only had fifty-two days left in America to figure out what to do.

Growing up in Singapore, she dreamed of working in New York. It was what she always wanted. She would say, "I can close my eyes and see myself down the road in five years: a stable, successful job, looking sharp in my black blazer by Prada (thanks to *The Devil Wears Prada*), and cool as a cucumber."

She would live a thrilling, jet-setting life: splitting her time between NY, London, and Singapore. But now that her job had fallen through, that vision wasn't going to happen. "Ah well," she thought, "I don't look great in black blazers anyways."

Now she had lots of time on her hands. "What should I do? Move to Singapore? Remain in NYC?" She had to figure out her next steps but had no career prospects or network. But . . . she still had her hopes and dreams. She knew what she wanted.

She realized she had to put herself out there. Yep, she was "on the market" once again. She needed a job and thought coffee chats could be the vehicle to help her find one. She reached out to anyone and everyone she knew to schedule a coffee chat and see what might happen. Since she didn't have a business network, she asked her professors, piano teacher, neighbors, hairdresser, friends, and friends' families if they knew anyone who might be willing to talk to her.

The idea of meeting people for coffee and getting to know them in a no-pressure, authentic way was such an American thing. During these coffee chats, she learned about their life stories, how they started their business. This is when she realized that *everyone* faces challenges: career changes, ups and downs, uncertainties.

Yet most of us are able to bounce back from our struggles and reinvent ourselves to achieve our dreams. We do this by valuing authenticity, the ability to choose what matters to us. Living authentically means you can trust yourself and your motivations. You can overcome obstacles such as losing your visa.

Then there is my dear friend Saleema Vellani. Saleema got the content of her own book and figured out through similar coffee chats a process she termed the "100 Coffee Challenge." This helped her build meaningful connections with people who are now not only her dear friends but also mentors, business partners, and clients. She said, "Strangely, ironically, I got to see who I really was, not who I thought I was, only by getting out there and interviewing people—not only the people who know me well but people who just met me!"

Put simply, authenticity means you're true to your own personality, values, and spirit, regardless of the pressure that you're under to act otherwise. You're honest with yourself and with others, and you take responsibility for what you want. Your values, ideals, and actions align. As a result, you come across as genuine, and you're willing to accept the consequences of being true to what you consider to be right.

It isn't always easy to live authentically. At times, being true to what is right means going against the crowd. It may mean being unconventional, opening yourself up for the possibility of others hurting you, and taking the harder road.

On one hand, it means missing some opportunities—you have to accept this. However, in the longer term, it's likely to open up many more opportunities—opportunities that simply wouldn't be available to someone who has been seen to be shifty, conflicted, vacillating, or inauthentic.

Living an authentic life is also vastly more rewarding than hiding your true self. When you live authentically, you don't have to worry about what you said (or didn't say), how you acted, or whether you did the right thing. Living authentically means you can trust yourself and your motivations implicitly.

Authenticity is another core value that leads to a life of satisfaction and meaningful purpose.

So now you have it. The key values that thousands agree are the foundation for living your best life.

BUSY-BUSTING TOOL #9

Values Vibrance

The clusters provide the basis for valuable and vibrant Values Vibing. Identifying your values and how you use them means acknowledging what's important to you. This simple exercise will help you complete what was set out in the chapter, supporting you in prioritizing depth, meaning, and satisfaction as core qualities of your life.

STEP ONE

Under each of the four core values, jot down a few things that come to mind when you think of that area. Don't think too long. Let it flow.

Connection	Energy	Growth Mindset	Authenticity

STEP TWO

Look back over your last week. Rate your performance in terms of living each value.

	Connection	Energy	Growth Mindset	Authenticity
Always				
Mostly				
Sometimes				
Rarely				
Never				

STEP THREE

Choose the value you scored lowest above. List three simple actions you can take to embrace this value better today.

For example: in terms of my example of Connection above:

 Spend one night per week doing something fun with my husband.
Go to yoga 3x next week. Ask one of the gals for coffee after.
Have my SheCAN! Community over to my house for a summer party.

STEP FOUR

Take those actions!

CHAPTER 10

ACCOUNTABILITY—SEAL THE DEAL

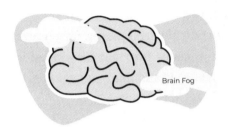

Brain Fog

I was intentionally busy. I had been living my dreams lately, doing so many amazing things—speaking engagements, rebranding campaigns, TV and radio interviews, and of course, writing this book. But something wasn't right. I felt like I was in a big brain fog. I was struggling more than usual to get things done.

What was going on? I felt like a bucket of ice water had just been poured over me. Me, the expert in Busy-Busting, was succumbing to Busyness again! Nope, not possible. I was living an intentional life working on things that mattered to me. After all, intentional Busyness isn't bad for me, right? Or is trying to fit five pounds of sugar in a three-pound canister just not a good idea? The extra two pounds need to go somewhere.

I decided, just for safety's sake, to run myself through the Busy Barometer.

I scored 64—not a good score. Yikes!

Did I make a mistake? Nope. A second run-through and my score was the same.

Now that I stopped to have a look, I could see it clearly. My schedule had become soooo full, and I'd been slipping back into BUSYNESS with not just a capital *B* but *all caps*!

But because it had been the most exciting time of my life, the endorphins were pumping and disguising it. I really loved the work I was doing. As a result, Busyness blindsided me. And this was frightening. Busyness was setting me up to take me out even while I was writing a book about busting it.

It was like being drunk while thinking I hadn't touched a drop and even leading AA meetings claiming to be sober the whole time.

And that, my friends, is the reality. In the substance abuse fellowships, they talk about their addict as a character, almost separate from them but living inside them. And I realize now that Busyness is similar. It is not something I can defeat and leave behind forever. I must always be vigilant.

When you're lost in the desert, an oasis is awesome stuff. But it is better to not be wandering in the dry sands in the first place. It is soooo easy to slip into old habits. And since delusion is at the heart of addiction, it's also easy to overlook it when it's happening. Until the next thing you know, you're eating cat food.

For me to put Busyness behind me once and for all, I had to come up with a way to always be alert when it might be creeping up on me from behind, to put guardrails around my recovery.

So I came up with the content of this chapter: accountability.

Accountability means putting clear, active measures in place to keep you on track. And although accountability is simple, it is not easy.

This chapter highlights a few techniques to ensure that, after you've bitten the Busyness bug, the Busyness bug doesn't bite you back. You can use them to augment the Busy-Busting Process.

Think of them as nuts on a hot fudge banana split. Remember, we go Beyond Busyness by taking the steps that work for us one microstep at a time. Here are a few more tips and tricks that work for me.

Tips to Be Accountable to Yourself

Track your values, not just your hours	Track your mojo, not just your results
Find partners - don't go at it alone	Take microsteps

ACCOUNTABILITY DEMANDS MEASUREMENT —TRACK YOUR VALUES, NOT JUST YOUR HOURS

Susan made a New Year's resolution to lose thirty pounds. She wanted to look better, feel better, and be better. She went on a radical diet, depriving herself from Monday through Friday of most of the foods she really liked.

Of course, that didn't work. On weekends, she binged on unhealthy food and skipped her runs. By the end of January, she hadn't lost even one pound, which is how they say 70 percent of New Year's resolutions go.

The problem was that like many yo-yo dieters, Susan was trying to lose weight and get fit using discipline alone. Her meal plan, personal trainer, and phone app—none of it solved this. She even joined an online group with members who had health goals similar to hers. Yet she kept struggling.

I advised her to try focusing on her values instead. What values did she care about that losing thirty pounds would support?

"Being healthy, of course," she answered. "Being energetic. Loving life. But also family. Being there for my kids."

"There you go," I said to her. "Focus on those."

By April, she had lost thirty pounds, and she had also run her first 5K race and received a clean bill of health from her doctor.

My input wasn't magic. It was simple common sense. Throughout history, people have tried to reach goals by measuring numbers only—and failing. The only way you can truly hold yourself accountable to a goal is to be clear how that goal aligns with your values—and then measure not just the results but also the actions you take to honor your values each and every day.

You can't be accountable for a goal because a goal only comes at the end. You can only be accountable to the daily actions that lead to it. But actions are not inspiring on their own. You need to be inspired first to take action. And you get inspired when the actions align with your values.

After the shock of scoring 64 when I thought everything was great, I took it upon myself to check back at the end of each day to see where I had spent my time. Each and every hour of the day, what goal had I dedicated it to? What results had I caused?

But the point isn't time management. It's value management. Was the way I spent my day aligned with my values?

Being accountable to living my values keeps me clear on my purpose, more self-aware, and resilient. It helps me make clearer and more powerful decisions. And of course, it gives me a sense of fulfillment even when I haven't yet reached my goals.

In alcohol addiction, recovery step 10 is about looking back at the day each evening and ensuring you have been living a life of recovery. Your behaviors, your thoughts, everything—are you staying on track? Are you living a values-driven life?

It takes me only ten minutes a day to note where I put my time for the entire sixteen hours I've been awake—and not just my work hours. Ten minutes. Yet the impact it creates is immense.

First, it allows me to identify which of the things I am doing that are not aligned with my values. Second, it provides an opportunity to defer, delete, or delegate. When my actions are focused, I get more accomplished, and it has more meaning.

ACCOUNTABILITY DEMANDS POSITIVE ENERGY —TRACK YOUR MOJO, NOT JUST YOUR RESULTS

Jessie wanted to be a realtor and make a full-time living but was struggling to make sales. She showed up to her biweekly group accountability sessions with her coach Cathay complaining about everything: COVID-19, the economy, her physical appearance, and mostly her teammates and clients. Soon, one of Cathay's other clients contacted her to say she couldn't listen to Jessie anymore—and neither could a lot of the other women in the group. They had begun to dread showing up at all.

So Cathay asked Jessie to impose a "silver lining policy" at her meetings. Any person wanting to complain had to flip the situation to make their statement positive. For instance, instead of Jessie saying, "The economy is making house sales impossible," Cathay coached her to say, "I realize that with the economy doing so poorly, interest rates are really favorable, and people who have liquid capital can get really good deals."

Soon, Jessie went from being "Negative Nancy" to "Joyful Jessie," bringing positivity and encouragement to every session. In fact, because she had the most complaints, Jessie became the greatest positive thinker. And indeed, Cathay asked her to track these flips. Jessie was flabbergasted to realize how much this simple technique changed her attitude—and her results as well.

The lesson? Accountability demands positivity. It's not only about doing what you said; it's about bringing great energy while doing it. Making sure you are practicing Mojo Making keeps your accountability fun and light.

Like measuring, it may seem annoying at first, but it's really easy and empowering. Make sure you look in the mirror often. If you notice you are not smiling, smile. Give yourself a mantra such as "I got this" or whatever floats your boat.

Libby Gill offers this helpful hack: "Set a timer for negativity. Like literally an egg timer or on your phone. Give yourself fifteen or twenty minutes for your very own pity party. Then when time's up, drop the negative attitude and pull yourself back up."

Remember, a great way to maintain your positive attitude is to implement happiness rituals. They are rituals because you do them regularly, ideally at the same time each day. Aligning them with mealtime, or waking and bedtime, or using alarms on your calendar, or putting up Post-it notes—all these techniques can help you ensure that you honor these rituals.

It's also important to remember to reward yourself and celebrate after you've done them. My last happiness ritual of the day, right before I do my inventory of the day, is celebrating the happiness rituals I have done the rest of the day before that.

When I put these rituals in place properly like that, they become nonnegotiables. And I always remember to include self-care in that. But as much as self-care is critical, also remember this: Mojo Making doesn't happen alone.

ACCOUNTABILITY DEMANDS PARTNERS —DON'T GO IT ALONE

Every morning Marie dragged herself out of bed at four thirty to study over a cup of coffee before her kids woke up for the day. Just one more year of this and she would get her master's degree in social work. All the hard work in night school would surely pay off eventually. But social work is taxing emotionally, on top of all the hours of study. One day she realized that she was miserable.

Then she thought, "I bet my classmates are feeling the same way. And maybe some of them are even up early struggling just like I am." She opened her computer and shot off an email, telling everyone she was opening an online conference room, and if anyone was available, they were invited to pop in and study with her.

To her surprise, four people showed up, despite the early hour. For the next forty-five minutes, they talked about their upcoming exam and admitted to one another the amount of stress they were feeling. It was clear to them that it was imperative to support one another if they wanted to succeed.

They continued to meet morning after morning, sometimes quizzing one another on class topics and sometimes just talking about what was on their to-do list for that day. Marie began to associate her master's degree with the joy she felt when she met with her classmates and looked forward to celebrating her wins with them and giving advice when they needed it the most.

On graduation day, she hugged every one of her group buddies tightly, almost in tears.

"You all kept me accountable when I would have slacked off," she said. "I couldn't have done this without you all."

They all agreed they couldn't have done it without her either, or one another. This shocked her to hear. She'd been so worried about herself she hadn't noticed that her partnership helped them as well.

Collaboration and communication make accountability far more powerful. Teamwork also provides different perspectives and a variety of potential checks and balances that help identify challenges before they become problems.

Helping others be accountable for the same thing you are doing gives you another layer of accountability for yourself and can help you feel you are part of a team even when you're doing something essentially alone.

Indeed, while I was writing my first book, I joined a group of friends and colleagues online to write together in what we call the Work Magic Room. We practice a technique called body doubling.

A body double is a friend or colleague who works at the same time as you, either in the same physical space or online. It doesn't matter what they are working on. Having other people working alongside us can help a lot with productivity because it helps us focus.

Yes, it provides teamwork and helps hold us to measurable goals. But it also keeps us firmly on track with what we intend. Working together keeps us focused.

We start off the session talking about our priorities, what we want to accomplish in the time together, and the steps we are taking to get it done. On the count of three, we begin working with our microphones on mute. Sometimes someone types something in the chat box, but typically everyone stays silent, very focused.

Knowing that others can see what I am doing, and watching them work with such incredible focus, keeps me focused. I achieve my goals 90% of the time with this group, a much higher percentage than I manage alone.

Again, it's not the teamwork itself that is the key to this success. It's the focus the teamwork brings me. I can't check emails or my Facebook while working in front of everyone. This drives my focus into flow levels. And when I'm focused like that, I cannot become busy again.

A LIFELONG COMMITMENT

Accountability, like busting Busyness, is not a one-time fix. It is a lifelong commitment to living a life aligned with our values, embracing positivity, and seeking support. By integrating these principles into our daily lives and being accountable for doing that, we can break free from the cycle of Busyness permanently and create a life of purpose and fulfillment.

So as you continue your journey of busting Busyness, always remember, let accountability be the guiding force that propels you to a life of balance, joy, and success. You have the power to create the life you desire, one step at a time. Embrace it, own it, and make it happen.

BUSY-BUSTING TOOL #10

Beyond Busy Report Card

Having a simple, easy-to-use report card will help you become both accountable and action-oriented. This simple check-in exercise can be done as often as you like. Simply ask yourself these two basic questions, each with three parts:

First part:

What one low-value activity do I tend to do, and am still doing, that I can immediately eliminate?

What mojo making activity can I replace it with starting today?

How can I ensure I keep doing that activity daily going forward?

Second part:

What core value of mine am I shortchanging again and again?

What activity can I take on to start living that value today?

How can I ensure I keep living that value every day?

Notice that the first part of both these questions requires you to identify where you are falling short, while the second part, in both, requires new and immediate action, and the third part looks at how to make the new action a habit. Past, present, future!

It is important to note that although Busyness might seem to be dominating your life, eliminating it starts with a single action. Small actions add up. Small actions, repeated one after the next, can quickly transform your entire life.

CHAPTER 11

AVOIDING RELAPSE

For the second week in a row, I couldn't sleep. I wasn't eating. I was mentally and physically burned out. My wick was as short as the one on the lilac-scented candle I hoped would soothe me. Instead, it melted all over my nightstand *and* destroyed both the nightstand and my new computer.

The mess freaked me out even more. Stress usually begets more stress. We lose control of our ability to focus, concentrate, and prioritize. I remember feeling the tears run down my cheek when I admitted to myself:

"My name is Peggy, and I am a Busyness addict who just fell off the wagon."

This time it felt different. It felt like my rock bottom. I was out of control, out of touch, and unable to function. I needed to find my feet again.

I took the next morning off to take stock. I had let my self-care slip out of control. I had taken on an impossible amount of work that sucked me into a vortex of eat, work, sleep, mother, repeat all over again.

Minus the mothering part. My son was thirty-two; he didn't need me in the same way he did twenty-eight years ago. And yet I was still drowning.

Then I realized what had thrown me off-balance. A close friend had committed suicide, and I blamed myself for it. I spent hours picturing her sitting by the river, taking those pills. I was drowning in guilt. It was a lifequake. I was not the same Peggy.

Staying in recovery from Busyness demands constant vigilance. Two-thirds of substance abusers in recovery relapse in the first year. That is a frightening fact.

There are no formal statistics for Busyness addiction, but I reckon the relapse rate is far worse because it's so acceptable. And there is no established Busyness recovery program. No network of recovering Busyness addicts. No big body of literature to read. I am very sure that all recovering Busyness addicts have suffered relapse.

Recovery is a lifelong process. That's why I wrote this book. Sharing these lessons with you has helped me cement the lessons into my consciousness. So I am adding this important chapter on relapse to help you cope with things when the pressure ratchets up.

SELF-VIGILANCE—BUSYNESS CONTROLLED ME UNTIL I LEARNED TO CONTROL IT

You now understand the causes and effects of Busyness. You know how Busyness works—inside, outside, and upside down. You know that Busyness is an addiction and that focusing on your values is the key to recovery. You have learned my Busy-Busting Process, and you hopefully have begun to implement it.

And like me, you may have already gone through a few cycles of relapse and recovery and come out stronger. And yet, like me, even if you have done all the above, you still need another level of strength.

Let me start with a confession of sorts. My relapses were preventable. While three-quarters of the population is stuck in a cycle of Busyness, I knew the way out. I spent three years developing the Busy-Busting Process. I was teaching others how but not practicing what I was teaching. I felt ashamed when I realized this. But hey, I am human.

With a lifetime of Busyness built into me, relapse is always just around the corner. It's not good enough to go through this process once. Or twice. It's not enough to even be writing a book on it and teaching people about it. Busy-Busting has to become a lifestyle of sorts. A conscious choice. This is your life. You have control over the choices you make.

But you don't live in a bubble. Life can be challenging. You have commitments and responsibilities. When life gets hard, tips and tricks are not enough.

The rest of this chapter offers strategies to cope when life feels out of control.

THE POWER OF SERENITY—LET GO OF CONTROL

Speaking of control. Rachel is a mother, wife, president of the PTA, and CEO of a marketing agency. For years she lived with what Buddhists call "monkey mind." Constantly unsettled, her brain was brimming with to-do lists.

One day she was helping her daughter Mia pack up for school while having a call with her work team. Toast was burning in the toaster, and her toddler, Bobby, was crying because she forgot to give him milk with his breakfast. A paper fell out of Mia's folder, and Rachel picked it up to tuck it back in.

"Don't worry, Mom," Mia said. "You don't have to sign that today. It's for the field trip to the zoo tomorrow, and since you're helping the class as a volunteer, obviously, I have your permission."

Rachel's mind quickly jumped back to the moment she had agreed, then jumped across to a vision of her calendar for tomorrow, crammed with meetings. She stared into Mia's face blankly as emails pinged on her phone.

Rachel knew at that moment that something had to change. She kissed Mia on the forehead, sent her off to school, and googled "How to get your mind in order." She came across thousands of pages filled with millions of tips. But the one that she immediately clicked on and opened began with "Let go . . ."

"My monkey mind made me think everything that passed in front of me was important," Rachel told me over coffee. "When I stopped for a minute to think about it, that's simply not true. There's a lot of stuff I can delegate to others. Other stuff I can ditch totally. I used to be terrified of trusting anyone or, worst of all, trusting my feeling that this thing could just be let go. Trust leads to the most prized thing in my life today—serenity."

Rachel had learned a lesson that was also hard-won for me. It's the ultimate key to recovery—let go. The ultimate power and energy in our lives comes from letting go.

If something is out of your control, there is nothing you can do about it no matter how much stress and drama you pour into it. All you can do is accept it and take it from there. As a friend of mine said, "If you spend your time on things you have no power over, you will lose 100 percent of the time." And this is the meaning of the Serenity Prayer:

God, grant me the serenity to accept the things I cannot change, the courage to change the things I can, and the wisdom to know the difference.

The Serenity Prayer has saved the lives of countless addicts. By God, the prayer is understood to mean any spiritual power you can find that is greater than you alone. It doesn't matter who that "God" is. What matters is that we ask for strength from outside ourselves when we feel our inner resources are not coping.

ASKING FOR HELP IS A POWER MOVE, NOT A WEAKNESS

Emma was a successful executive, running her own marketing agency. Her days were full. Usually, she stayed on top of her workload. But lately, she was feeling overwhelmed. Despite her best efforts, her to-do list seemed to grow longer each day, and she was struggling to find time for self-care and family.

Then the overwhelm started impacting her work. She found herself making mistakes, losing documents, and forgetting deadlines. And missing important appointments. Something needed to change, or the business she worked so hard to develop would melt away. She would lose what she worked so hard to make happen.

Emma called a team meeting. She explained to her staff how she was feeling and admitted she needed help. She laid out specific tasks she wanted to delegate: research, data analysis, content creation. Her team was eager to jump in and help. It didn't happen right away; she needed to train them and realize no one would do things the way she would. They would do it differently, sometimes better but sometimes not as well as she could do herself.

Asking for help took the extra weight off Emma's shoulders, and her company began to soar again. At the same time, her personal life came back as well. All because she just asked for help.

Asking for help is a simple solution when you're under pressure. But for most of us, it doesn't come easily at all. If you struggle to ask for help, I completely understand. Me, I'm independent. Thanks, but no thanks. I'll handle it myself. Besides, no one can possibly do it to the standard I want, and it will take longer to explain than to do it myself.

Somewhere along the line, I took on the belief that asking for help equates to weakness. What poppycock. No one ever achieved anything important by themselves. A painter needs her gallerist. A book writer needs her editor.

Asking for help is, in fact, a great sign of strength. It takes a strong person to be able to speak up. Even Superman and Wonder Woman need support from trusted sidekicks and allies. And they are cartoon characters who have powers beyond those of human beings. So it is really absurd to be ashamed as a human being to ask for someone to walk alongside you.

> **Playbook for Asking for Help**
>
> ☐ Acknowledge that you need help.
>
> ☐ Identify what kind of help you need. Be very clear about this. Do you need someone to help you with specific tasks? Do you need emotional support?
>
> ☐ Speak up. Be clear and direct. Don't drop hints or beat around the bush.
>
> ☐ Provide sufficient background information so the person helping you can understand the situation.
>
> ☐ Trust the process. Be open and receptive to the person's response. They may not be able to help in the way that you think you need. But their solutions might actually work out better. Believe the help you seek is actually going to work out.
>
> ☐ Be grateful! This can be as simple as saying thank you. Or maybe you can do something helpful for the person who helped you.
>
> ☐ Acknowledge their support. They deserve to be made a hero - if they want to. But this acknowledgment doesn't have to be public - you could simply thank them privately as well. Find out how they feel about you sharing about their generosity.

SOMETIMES THE BEST WAY TO FIND A COMMUNITY IS TO MAKE ONE

I left my job at United Health to take care of my father. When he passed away, I didn't want to get back to work too fast. I was thinking about my own mortality. I was pondering what was the purpose of my life. How am I making a difference? What unique things could I do that would have real value to those around me?

One of my dad's core mantras was "Work hard. Be humble. Every day is a gift. And the best gift is giving back."

His mantra kept echoing through my mind in the weeks that followed his passing. I didn't want to go back to the corporate world. I wanted to do something that would help women like myself navigate the challenges of juggling career, family, and personal development.

Dad was a bit of a loner. But even he used to go to play bridge every day in his later years. He called it his "bridge community." When he didn't go, he missed it—and the people at the coffee shop missed him. It kept him vital right until the end.

At first, I considered buying a service-oriented franchise. But none of the options I researched represented a mission and vision I was interested in: focus on every aspect of the total woman—give them the tools to be successful.

When I was in the thick of navigating my career, most of my mentors were men who truly didn't understand the roadblocks busy women face. But more importantly, they didn't know the shortcuts that would make things easier and set them up for success. I did not have a community that was focused on my personal and professional success. I did not have a supportive group to keep me positive or just vibe with. Then the lightbulb went off. It wasn't just my problem but a challenge that so many other women faced.

So I decided to start my own organization. I've already told you about it: SheCAN! It is actually named after my dad: Ted Kahn. Get it? Well, maybe not so obvious. It started off as SheKahn, but no matter how hard I tried to get that name to stick, the members kept falling back to SheCAN!

Building SheCAN! was no easy feat. It took many meetings with lawyers and extensive education on starting a 501(c)(3). Then came the job of assembling the board of directors. I wanted them all to be female, and I didn't know enough of the right kind of women locally, so that was also tough.

I pulled out *Business First*'s book of lists and scoured the pages to find the most influential women in the area and started making phone calls. The result was a group of a dozen powerhouse women from all personal and professional backgrounds, and it was then that I started feeling the sense of community that I was striving to create. This was a community I had been looking for most of my life.

We started doing research into the issues that most concern women. At that point I started to realize how busy every woman is. And that was when I started to see the extent of the Busyness addiction.

SheCAN! has grown into a loving community that has one another's backs. One way we support one another is to help one another stop from relapsing to Busyness. When women go to SheCAN! events and hear all these stories from other women who have overcome something challenging, it makes it so much easier for the rest of us.

Studies show that being a member of a community reduces your risk of cardiovascular disease and mental health issues. People with a group of like-minded individuals around them have a 50 percent less risk of death when ill than those with fewer social relationships. Social isolation rivals smoking, obesity, and physical inactivity as a negative health indicator. It increases the risk of dementia by 50 percent; leads to more depression, anxiety, and suicide; and worsens heart disease and strokes by nearly a third.

I am not saying you have to register a nonprofit organization to help you avoid relapse or cope with challenging situations. You don't even have to build a community at all. You can make a list of people you know who you can draw on for support. You can get them together as a group. Or you can just go out and find existing groups and communities to become part of.

The point is, however you do it, the power of community is a support system that is extremely valuable. If asking one friend for help is effective, consider how much more effective a community of dozens is. Communities get you out of your head. At church or synagogue, all those pressures you thought were crushing you become unimportant.

Carolyn Gitlin travels the world speaking about connection and community. "Community fuels my soul," she told me. "When my parents got divorced, I was still very young. It was the community around us that helped me survive that."

LOOK BACK AT YOUR ACCOMPLISHMENTS
AND REMEMBER YOU'VE DONE IT BEFORE

Natasha owns a chain of coffee shops and has a team of employees. But lately, she never seems to get to the end of her work. No matter who she has hired, no matter how much she delegates, it just seems to get harder and harder, with her to-do list spilling out the edges of her computer monitor like some kind of tidal wave. She has started having panic attacks, something she hasn't experienced since her divorce, nearly a decade ago.

So the other day, Natasha stopped. She took some deep breaths and thought back to that earlier time when she had felt this way. The divorce was a full-fledged lifequake.

She called back some of the techniques she used then. She took a deep breath and started to make a plan, adapting the tools she had already mastered to the current situation. It took only a few days before her life felt back in control. The memory of this victory in the past empowered Natasha now.

Any time I have faced a challenge in my life, what has often gotten me through it is remembering how I dealt with similar challenges in my past. It's a huge confidence boost when you remember that the situation is not new at all.

And the great thing about relapse is this is always true. By definition, relapse means you have already overcome the addiction at least once. The memories of how I triumphed over it last time can either become a way to scold myself for falling back into the trap or an elixir to empower me to get back on that horse. Not a hard choice.

BUSY-BUSTING TOOL #11

Recovery Is a Lifelong Challenge

Our ability to rise above addiction is a learned skill. When faced with challenges, we often slip into autopilot and revert to obsessive and compulsive behavior.

○○○

Think about the hardest challenges you have faced. Write a few of them down.

1.	
2.	
3.	
4.	
5.	

○○○

What did you do to overcome them (for example: broke them into small steps, or got help from people who have had this challenge before)? List the things you have previously done that helped.

Remember how it felt in the thick of it and how you felt when you nailed it. Envision and bring back those feelings.

CHAPTER 12

YOUR NEW MANTRA—LESS IS MORE

My front tooth fell into my morning coffee.

I was on the road, in Washington, DC, filming a speech at the World Trade Bank and doing a work sprint and photo shoot with my publisher for this book.

This day of all days required having an intact set of front teeth. Not just for cosmetic reasons but because my ability to speak clearly without a front tooth was a challenge: my words were garbled. When I was in a panic, trying to talk with my out-of-town dentist about viable options, which included supergluing my tooth back in, I realized I was hard to understand. My dentist kept on asking me to repeat myself because she couldn't understand me. How would a room full of people?

Since time was short, I sent a photograph of my mouth to two local dentists. Both confirmed they could not repair it. And as much as I am a fan of microsteps that allow for immediate action, neither dentist could suggest any such step. And I couldn't think of anything either, short of supergluing my tooth back in, but that was not even a viable option because there was nothing to glue it too, but I still tried.

Of course, I was obviously embarrassed to have my tooth missing on such an important day. But it represented something else far worse. I had spent the last year and a half rebuilding my mouth and jawbone with dentures, bridges, crowns, dental implants, and bone grafts. It was an immense investment of time, money, and effort. And now this was happening? COVID-19 destroyed the health of my jawbone. To save my teeth and capacity for implants, I needed over fourteen bone grafts.

Bone grafting is a surgical procedure that aims to create a solid base for dental implants where the existing jaw lacks sufficient natural bone due to things such as tooth loss, gum disease, or deterioration of the jaw itself over time.

As you can imagine, this procedure can be shockingly painful. Of course, it is usually performed under anesthesia. The dentist or oral surgeon makes an incision in the gum and places bone graft material in the slit. Then they close the gum with stitches. It takes three to six months for the jaw to heal enough to allow the dentist to place the implant.

So you can see that as much as I was worried about missing my talk and my book shoot, there was a much bigger issue at stake. The pain, the cost, the inconvenience—I could not bear the thought of yet another operation. Or worse, several operations. But it looked like that was exactly what was in store for me.

Because with a front tooth missing, so much gets compromised. But worse, for me it was the sign of longer-lasting challenges.

BUSYNESS IS A PANDEMIC

This situation with my tooth reminded me of my experience during COVID-19. It's an experience many of us suffered. No matter how much we worked to overcome a tough situation, it just seemed to get worse. One lockdown followed another, a relentless series of revisions that brought the world to one standstill after the next.

The world suffered a trauma that shut us down physically and emotionally as we shifted to meet a new reality. Each time we reacted to the updated situation, it seemed to change yet again. For most of us our physical and mental wellness plummeted while our relationships fell apart. We were unable to live the lives we had become used to.

Strangely, COVID-19 made us both more and less prone to the addiction of Busyness. For me, my work depended on face-to-face events that came to a screeching stop. For someone like me who values so greatly spending time with my relatives, family, and friends, and both creating and being part of communities, COVID-19 was not only challenging, but it was also downright depressing.

With all this free time, you would think being busy would be almost impossible. And yet like many people, I found myself as busy as ever. First, of course, having to readjust how my business worked took a lot of hard trial-and-error effort, which took a lot more time than doing what I knew.

But it was more than that. When I started to pay attention, I noticed that I simply expanded what I needed to do to fill the hours I had available. And I also noticed that other people were doing it too.

Sure, some of us had to deal with managing child care or taking care of our parents or working from home when there was no equipment or space. This was extremely stressful and legitimately added to our workload. And yes, we had to take many more precautions that took up precious hours, such as sanitizing everything in sight or hunting for toilet paper when every grocery store was barren.

Then there was the loneliness and isolation. When I walked down the street in the early days of the pandemic, I was saddened by how we all kept our heads down, avoiding eye contact as if our mere glances were contagious. I couldn't see people's expressions behind their masks. And it was like we hid our eyes to match this masking. This was an emotion, nonphysical masking, pretending that everything was OK or, at the very least, would be at any moment.

How long would we have to force this positivity? How long would we keep treading water with no shore in sight?

I realize that Busyness is like COVID-19. It's more than just a personal bad habit. It's a collective affliction, a contagion that rips through the culture like a virus.

It begins as innocuously as a sneeze, one person juggling too much telling another, "I'm so busy!" and making the other person envious, like one alcoholic bragging to another about their barhopping hijinks.

Like COVID-19, Busyness has a ripple effect. If I am busy, you, my colleague or close friend, need to be busier: more productive (myth), more present in more things (myth), more successful (straight-up lie).

And like COVID-19, the results are predictable, though varying in their severity.

Busyness compromises our health and brings us exhaustion and stress just like COVID-19 does. Along the way, it damages our relationships, our connection to other people, and our happiness, just like lockdown did.

Both the pandemic and Busyness have short-term and long-term consequences.

THE BEST VACCINE

This book has taught a process that could be considered both a treatment for Busyness and its vaccine. Whether you're pro or con vaccines, applied to a busy life, the Busy-Busting Process should help you, without doubt, cure yourself of the Busyness addiction and get on the road to recovery. (Remember, you are never fully recovered, always in process.)

At the same time, though, many of the elements of the process are critical to maintaining your new, less busy life. You might never have taken a moment to understand the elements that compose your COVID-19 vaccines or how they work. Or maybe you have. Either way, I do want to make sure you understand the pieces that comprise your Busyness vaccine because they will help you prevent yourself from getting sick again and having your teeth fall out (again, just a metaphor there).

This section is designed to just remind you of what you've already read, a review of the most important elements, not as part of the process but just as reminders of ways of being that encourage you to stay not too busy.

Self-awareness is, of course, number one. Recognize when Busyness is becoming a default state. Are you over-committed? Are you sacrificing your well-being for the sake of getting it all done? Are you trying to be superhuman, showing off how important you are not only to others but to yourself as well?

Prioritizing your values is of massive importance. When you focus on what truly matters to you, you find it easier to say no to commitments that do not align with your values. More importantly, it ignites your happiness muscle because you're spending your time on what matters to you.

Set boundaries. There is space for things other than work. And you don't have to manage your personal life as if it was your company. You can actually take time to think, plan, or just push your reset button. You can ignore your communication alarms and notifications most of the time, but one tiny word—no—can create universes of space in your life.

Disconnection. We have focused on connecting to other humans who matter to you. Now we're adding this: Make sure you disconnect from everything else. Whether it's technology or time being sucked away by people who are not out for your best interests, unplugging can, ironically, make it easier and more powerful to connect.

Single task. Rather than multitasking, do one thing at a time. It may *feel* or seem like this is ineffective. But measure it. Check how much more effective single tasking can be in terms of results *and* how much more pleasant it is.

Seek support. When you fall back into Busyness, it can be hard to even notice. Create accountability partnerships to help others help you notice when you are taking on too much. Share your strategies on how to be more intentional. Communicate with other like-minded busy individuals who understand the busy traps we get stuck in.

Mindfulness. Remember my cat food story when I accidentally gobbled a mouthful of pet food thinking it was pistachio nuts? Being in a mindless haze from burnout makes you do dumb things such as feed the cat pistachio nuts and eat cat food. Slow down to be more productive. Rest and intention will improve your performance because you will act with more purpose.

Celebrate small victories. I cannot emphasize this enough: Microsteps.

Stay calm. This may be the most important element of all. What often drives Busyness is a sense that we are under pressure and have to get certain things done. This can be underlying and hidden or quiet on the surface. It can be explicit, such as the result of a specific deadline or job, or it can be implied, such as when we just feel we have to achieve more.

Do not underestimate the difficulty of getting Busyness "under control." It took two years to get COVID-19 managed, and Busyness has been around about a million times longer. I imagine one of the first sentences prehistoric hominids uttered was "I'm so busy!" furrowing their robust, bony brow ridge with frustrated pride.

You cannot get Busyness under control in any easy, predictable way. My Busy-Busting Process can help, and it is important thereafter to stay vigilant, prioritize your values, be accountable, and stay relaxed. *If finding serenity seems like more willpower than you can muster, I have a recommendation for you.*

FAST TRACK TO CALM AND PEACE

Finding tranquility can seem impossible for most of us. It's not like a switch you can turn on and off. But what if there was a ten- to twenty-minute microexercise available when and where you need it? There is, and it's an app with superpowers. Say hello to Sensate, an immersive experience created through the power of infrasonic resonance paired with soundscapes. The beauty is you don't have to do anything to feel the relaxing impact.

If you're like me and had no clue what infrasonic resonance is, here's is a low-tech description. It refers to low-frequency vibrations that occur at rates below the range of human hearing. While generally inaudible, their vibrational energy can still be sensed and provide profound calm in the moment, reduce stress, and improve resilience over time. I've been using it a lot lately, and it has been my go-to tool for when I need to slow down and quiet the noise, *a fast track to calm and peace.*

Using it is effortless. You just put what looks like a two-inch by three-inch egg-shaped pebble on your chest, turn on the app, and listen to the soundtracks that are specifically synchronized with the vibration for what feels like a big slice of tranquility. It uses the natural resonance of sound waves in the chest to calm the body's vagus nervous system, facilitating instant relief and long-term benefits with regular use, such as improved sleep and the ability to relax and focus after a ten-minute session.

The vagus nerve is a long nerve that originates in the brain stem and extends through the neck into the chest and abdomen. It is tasked with regulating critical body functions such as heart rate, blood pressure, breathing, and digestion. It also controls the sympathetic nervous system, which handles "fight or flight" responses. When you stimulate the vagus nerve, it provides sensory information to the skin and muscles, which, in turn, helps you eliminate stress.

Less stress means more productivity, and that is far more reliable than trying to be more productive by being busy (which by now you know does not work at all).

I got turned on to this technology by my friend Mary Hendra, who just changed jobs to work at Sensate. She is a big advocate of aligning with a purpose-driven organization and puts quality of life at the top of her list. The Sensate product uses technology to reduce stress. This is a fascinating concept I found unbelievable until I used it myself.

It is pretty remarkable in the way it has reduced my stress, improved my mood, and facilitated deep sleep and creative thinking. I met the founder, Anna Gudmundson, when I was interviewing thought leaders for this book. In her words,

> *Running a tech start-up is extremely taxing. In most cases, in order to build technology so that you can get revenue, you depend on other people's money. You're constantly trying to do everything, building products, raising money, running a team, structuring marketing plans, etc., while having too little time, funds, people, or resources. I think the biggest challenge is to manage*

your energy. The early stage of a start-up is like a sprint and a marathon at the same time.

So it's the juggling of a million things while making sure that you're in your best possible mental shape to do the job. Body included. Many burn out, and I'd rather someone quit than get to that point. I've been there myself a couple of times in previous jobs.

The challenging part of a start-up is the pace and the pressure. It's just not for everyone. The typical tech start-up journey is tough. But life is tough for many. They need help to unwind, relax, and get a good night's sleep or spur your creative juices. This is why we created the Sensate technology and the easy access to it.

I have been using the Sensate daily, and it has changed my life in a profound way. I am not a big advocate for promoting products, but if you are looking for something that will stop the noise and improve your performance, this is the ultimate gadget.

Get smart! If you can't find time for a full gym session, try microexercise instead. Likewise, if you don't have time for a yoga retreat, supercharge your relaxation with a Sensate session!

SUBTRACTION

In a *New York Times* opinion piece,[*] climber Francis Sanzaro explained how his failure at a difficult ascent was caused by his aspiration to get to the top.

---

[*] Francis Sanzaro, "When I Stopped Trying to Self-Optimize, I Got Better," *New York Times*, September 17, 2023, https://www.nytimes.com/2023/09/17/opinion/sports-zen-mental-subtraction.html.

It is a strange dichotomy. Visualizing himself at the top of the mountain—a technique every motivational coach suggests—didn't get him there. Near the peak, he fell. By imagining his success, he had bound himself with it, made it part of his self-image. The pressure became greater, not less. It created an unconscious and unavoidable performance anxiety.

As soon as he gave up his desire to succeed at the climb, it became fun. He was able to joyfully scramble up the cliff face without incident.

He had discovered, he wrote, the Power of Subtraction. Allow him to explain it in his own words:

> *When I added (determination, grit, self-confidence, desire), I failed. When I took away (the desire for success), my body moved with greater fluidity and naturalness. I improved. I enjoyed it more as well.*

He goes on to then say something truly profound:

> *The tactic of subtraction goes against the grain of the so-called mindset revolution, in which it seems everyone is adding this or that quality to their mental approach. The growth mindset. The abundance mindset. The gratitude mindset. But in this genre of self-optimization, if it can be called that, we are adding more and more duct tape to something that isn't broken—our mind— until it is so covered we lose sight of the beautifully designed machine underneath it all and it thus becomes, in fact, broken.*

To me, this sounds an awful lot like Busyness.

The glorification of more.

The sanctification of adding one more task, technique, or desired result.

The belief that the only way to get more is to try for more. Do extra stuff. Do the reps.

I mean, it makes logical sense.

But it doesn't work out.

You know this because you've tried it, and it has never worked.

You're left exhausted and burned out. And you didn't get what you strived for.

Try subtraction instead.

It improves your ability to focus, to be present.

Get more by doing less.

I've already showed you how.

More is less.

Less is more.

Now get out there and show the world what we're talking about.

A NEW, IMPROVED ME

I walked into the grocery store and was looking at my shopping list when I felt someone tap me on the shoulder and say, "Peggy Sullivan, is that you?"

I turned around to find a friend I hadn't seen in over eight months. I was thrilled to see her, and we quickly got lost in catch-up conversation.

When we got done with the small talk, she looked me straight in the eye and said, "I barely recognize you. You have also lost quite a bit of weight? You look relaxed, happy, and healthy and obviously loving the life you're living. I am so proud of your writing and speaking."

All of it made me feel good, but I couldn't understand what she meant by the weight loss comment and me looking so different. I have been the same 110 pounds for over twenty years.

We got back together a couple of weeks later for a glass of wine. She said it again: "You are so different."

I had to ask what she was talking about as I hadn't lost any weight.

She said not physical weight but mental weight. "Like the weight of the world just got removed from your shoulders. Don't overthink it, but whatever you're doing lately, it looks really good if you keep it up."

It was then I realized what she meant. My always-on lifestyle led me in every direction but the one I truly wanted to follow. I wasn't healthy, happy, or focused on what's important. I lost my ability to smile, and when I did, it came off as forced. I was always thinking about the next thing on my never-ending list, never allowing myself to enjoy life in the moment. How this came to become a metaphorical weight on my shoulders, I don't know, but it seems that I was blind to it while others saw it clearly.

These days I can't stop smiling. I smile when loading the dishes. I hum when vacuuming. Even when addressing a thorny work issue, I never allow myself to get so frustrated that it steals my joy. I know how to keep myself accountable so that relapses are few and far between. What's more, I know that one day I am going to celebrate one decade and maybe even two without slipping into Busyness once. But there are busy traps all around me, so I must remain vigilant.

And now you can too. I hope my research and my stories have helped you see this powerful, simple truth:

You can choose meaning over mayhem.

You can do less to accomplish more.

You can do less to become more.

You can go Beyond Busyness and live a life of meaning and joy.

Remember, a journey of a thousand miles begins with the first *micro*step.

The opposite of busy is making conscious, intentional choices. The world Beyond Busyness is waiting for you, and it feels ****ing amazing.

So let's get going.

CALL TO ACTION

Want to join a community that will support you in achieving more with less? Need tips and tricks on how to move beyond busy? Tired of Busyness holding you back? Or maybe you just want to hang with like-minded people who value what's really important in life. Go to **peggysullivanspeaker.com/beyond-busyness**.

ACKNOWLEDGMENTS

I want to thank the following:

All of my value-driven cohorts, who not only inspire but also remind me of what is truly important: helping others step into their possibility and making the world a better place one microstep at a time.

Tom Sullivan, my husband, for loving me unconditionally even when I am a hot mess. You are my rock!

Brandon Fink, my son who makes me proud every day for his brilliance, love of life, and ability to be at the top of his game professionally while leading a balanced life. So proud of you and grateful we can bounce our thought leadership off each other.

Chelsea Demby, my son's better half, for making him a better man.

My dad, Ted Kahn, who taught me I can do hard things and gave me a mantra to live life by. I can hear him say, "Toots, a day without learning something new is a lost opportunity." He dedicated his life to growth as a core value and showed me how we can rise up to any challenge when we are willing to learn.

My mom, Suzanne Kahn, who told me, "Happiness is your responsibility." It is not a thing or a destination that I will be happy when I reach it but a series of small choices made every day. On the last days of her life, when death was near, she chose to joyfully live in the moment and be thankful. Inspiration at its best.

David Meerman Scott, my mentor for making everything I do stronger and relentlessly reminding me that family and fun are choices we can and should make for ourselves daily.

Nick Morgan, communications coach and theorist, author, keynote speaker, *Harvard Business Review* and *Forbes* blogger, for teaching me how to be a better speaker and wanting to help others how to step into their personal power.

ImpactEleven, my speaking community who teaches me every day to level up, and we are better together, so give generously and never keep a scorecard.

Josh Linkner, fellow speaker, author, and creative thinking guru who is a master at his craft. He has taught me so much not only professionally but also personally, as he is an individual who cherishes family and always makes room for them. He is a legend, and legends do the work.

Amplify Publishing—Naren, Brandon, and Jess, for taking me on when I needed help. Your kindness, knowledge, and attention to detail are outstanding.

Saleema Vellani, founder of Ripple Impact, author, speaker, entrepreneur, and soulmate. Your courage and passion to always tell people what they need to hear, not what they want to hear is so refreshing and valued. In today's world where so many relationships are about "what's in it for me," you give relentlessly.

The Women of Ripple Impact (Amna, Walija, Malaya, Tanjina, and Zainab), for supporting me no matter how much time or energy it takes to get it as good as it can be. Your ability to stay curious about how to get the job done and seriously move the needle makes each of you the best working partner anyone could have.

Michael Lee, for helping me write a witty book with strong thought leadership.

Michelle Markey, my right- and left-hand support system. Thank you for showing other women the superpowers of a single mom. Your ability to operate at the highest point of contribution regardless of life's daily distractions is commendable.

Ashley Falletta, for working by my side through so many marketing challenges.

Germain Santana, advertising executive at Google, who leads his people by example and taught me the power of persistent networking. I will never forget the talk we did for your Google team. You give 100 percent to support your team, and that makes you a very effective leader.

Tina Sula, a friend and one of the wisest women I know who has been there with unconditional support over the years. I will never forget how you shared my first book with your network of hundreds at your personal expense. You wrote the book on friendship and what real support looks like.

Christina Allessi, founder and managing director of Sfera Speaking Bureau. You consistently remember to lead a life where your values are the filter for every decision. Thank you for supporting me and waiting till the timing was right for both of us.

Aunt Adrienne, for being a mother of sorts after my mom died young. Through thick and thin, you support me and call me the daughter you have never had. It's a privilege.

MaryAnne Cappon, a thirty-five-year friend who reminds the world how a positive attitude and smile can both empower us and brighten everything.

Paula Dobozin, one of my besties who has shown me how the power of humor and fun improve every situation. I will never forget Costa Rica and the Betsy Ross incident. You have taught me transformation is a North Star, and it's the journey, not the destination.

Dani and Joe, my trainers at Fitch Fitness, for giving me the joy of exercise and good health. You have a way of inspiring your community to greater heights that is rare. Keep it up.

The Menzas (Terry, Frank, Aly), who show me daily what unconditional family love looks like. Blood is thicker than water.

All the people I interviewed for your valuable perspective:

David Meerman Scott, bestselling author, entrepreneur, and speaker

Erik Qualman, a political speaker, bestselling author of social comics, digital leader

Lauren Simonetti, Fox News correspondent, podcast host

Michael Ashford, podcaster, TEDx, senior director at The Receptionist

Carolyn Gitlin, Jewish Federation of North America's National Women's Philanthropy Division

Madelyn Blair, PhD, teacher at Columbia University, resilience leader, author

German Santana, head of revenue, analytics and optimization, local news, global partnerships, and apprentice manager at Google

Libby Gill, eight-time author, speaker, entrepreneur, thought leader

Dr. Meg Scherer, PhD, VP of HR, Citi Bank

Mary Hendra, VP of development, American Way

Paula Dobozin, outside sales manager, G-Tech Bus Parts

Skyler Sorkin, founder, host of *Regardless* podcast, senior account executive at Influential

Tamara McMillan, CEO-founder of Empower MEE, social scientist, speaker, thought leader

Jon Westover, professor of organizational leadership, podcast host for *Human Capital Leadership*, editor

Kate Glaser, founder of Hope Rises, consultant, TV personality

Amani Fancy, Olympic champion figure skater, *Dancing on Ice* winner, head of growth at Ripple Impact

Dr. Miriam Zylber, mental health physician, doctor at a leading Miami hospital, wellness expert, author

Carla Johnson, innovation architect, ten-time author, global keynote speaker

Tina Sula, director of philanthropic development, Jewish Federation

Ana Isabel Nobia, NBC morning show host—Miami

Shane Rye, therapist for Miami Dolphins

Gloria Burns, writer-podcaster for Miami newspapers

Andy Alsop, the brainchild of Employee Supremacy, CEO of The Receptionist

Everyone who beta-read my book: David Meerman Scott, Libby Gill, Saleema Vellani, MaryAnne Capon, Paula Dobozin,

Tina Sula, Skylar Sorkin, Julie Zhu, Ashley Falletta, Michelle Markey, Carolyn Gitlin, Kristina Strobel, Victoria Brooks, Sue Freed, and Daniel Hore.

ABOUT THE AUTHOR

Peggy Sullivan is a corporate performance expert, author, entrepreneur, and keynote speaker.

With her signature blend of lively storytelling, heartfelt vulnerability, and laugh-out-loud humor, she has inspired organizations of all kinds from all over the world, including Google, Bank of America, Merrill Lynch, and Blue Cross Blue Shield.

Her data-driven strategies for organizational transformation and personal empowerment have been featured in *Forbes*, *Inc.*, *Time*, *Bloomberg Businessweek*, and *Entrepreneur*, as well as on Fox, CBS, and NBC.

As founder and CEO of the national women's nonprofit SheCAN!, she was awarded the New York Women in Leadership award and the Marketing 2.0 Outstanding Leadership award.

She is also the author of *Happiness Is Your Responsibility*, an actionable tool kit for reclaiming your inner joy.